BUNMI ASAOLU

Surviving SAJOMACO

A Nigerian Boarding School Odyssey

Twenty twenty, your boy turned forty
Nigeria turned sixty
A giant gone awry
Makes me want to sigh, cry?
Haba

My two scores ensconced in its three
Said goodbye once, but it can't leave me
And so began the excavating
The first half of the nineties, the making
Of me

OAU Ife to SAJOMACO
Clean swap, head down, lay low
How clueless I was
Even in boarding school, Naija showed us
Pepe

For the SAJOMACO 1996 set.

Contents

Preface

After graduating from my boarding school, St. John/Mary's Unity Secondary School (aka SAJOMACO), in 1996, my parents uprooted our family from Ile-Ife, Nigeria, to London because the country had shown us all enough *pepe*[1]. When parents evade straightforward questions from their children about one-way tickets to London, you know something is amiss. And try to convince young impressionable minds that a tiny fifth-floor council flat in pre-gentrified Hackney, London isn't so far removed from a spacious duplex and open fields in Ile-Ife.

During those initial weeks after arriving in London, I spent an inordinate amount of time processing my SAJOMACO years, especially the final year, which showed the best and worst aspects of my boarding school. But there were A Levels and a university degree to obtain, and a career to build. So, the writing took a backseat.

Years later, while discussing my school experiences with my wife, Tosin, I insisted that we (SAJOMACO graduates) weren't traumatised by them. But I still wonder why I felt the urge to start documenting those experiences immediately after arriving in London. Maybe it was therapy after all.

My recollection of events at SAJOMACO is not perfect. It is

---

[1] Hot cayenne pepper.

also predominantly from a boy's perspective in a mixed school. From the limited conversations I have had with a few of our female classmates, their experiences appeared to be worse. I accept that not everyone will agree with the accounts as I have laid them out or with my perspectives, but I have tried to give a faithful account of the events as much as possible. I excluded some stories because I chose to focus on one theme: survival against the odds.

After leaving SAJOMACO, my classmates and I were hopeful that life would be better for future generations of students. Today, that hope is like a counterfeit kerosene lantern's wick. An aerial shot of the school grounds is a sorry sight to behold. Even to an untrained eye, one can easily make out the outline of classroom buildings that have been reclaimed by nature.

Ultimately, *Surviving SAJOMACO* is about reflection. As the Yoruba say, *'Agba ki i wa l'oja k'ori omo tuntun wo'*[2]. From a teenager's perspective at the time, our teachers were the adults in the proverbial room. It was not my intention to demonise them. If my accounts paint some of them as tyrants, that's because I chose not to sugar-coat their behaviour, which was amplified by aspects of Nigerian culture that I am not proud of. I should add that many of our teachers were committed to their job and a few were angels.

In retrospect, I realise that our teachers were also fighting their own survival battles. However, shouldn't some soul-searching lead to some truth-telling? If Nelson Mandela was right – that the youth of today are leaders of tomorrow, then dysfunctional school systems of today will produce

---

[2] An elder will not be around in the market while the head of a newborn is left to dangle dangerously.

dysfunctional leaders of tomorrow. The fact is our surviving carried on beyond SAJOMACO because outside those school gates lay an even greater challenge – that of surviving in Nigeria. Now, that would take a library's worth of memoirs.

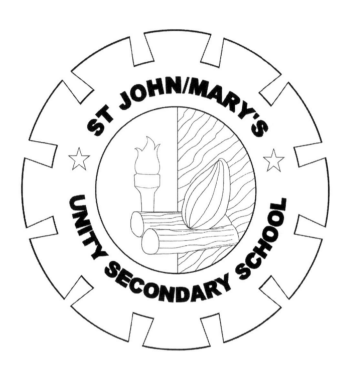

SAJOMACO MAP

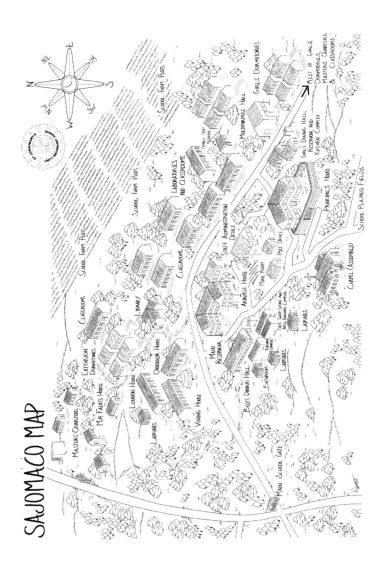

I

Part One | Immersion

'But they could neither of them persuade me, for there is nothing dearer to a man than his own country and his parents, and however splendid a home he may have in a foreign country, if it be far from father or mother, he does not care about it.'
— *Homer*

Chapter 1

Before my older brother, Wolex, moved up in life by starting secondary school, the concept of boarding school was not part of my reality. There were none in Ile-Ife, south-west Nigeria, where we lived.

I grew up on Obafemi Awolowo University campus, often referred to simply as OAU. It was peaceful and boasted beautiful scenery. Truth be told, it was such a bubble that some people were born, raised and educated on the university grounds, with limited interaction with the world outside the campus. In fact, a few ended up working as lecturers at the university after graduating.

Our early taste of life outside this comfort zone came in the fourth year of primary school, when some of our classmates at the University Staff School began to complement the teaching at school with private tuition.

Mum was usually the one to try out new things. She was the risk-taker. Dad was super-conservative. The differences between them can be explained by their upbringing – Mum was more exposed, having grown up in the more developed Ibadan, an hour's drive from Ile-Ife, while Dad was raised on the farm, in a small village close to Ilesha, about forty-five minutes' drive in the opposite direction.

Despite that, Dad was the more educated of the two, eventually ending up at the University of Cambridge to study for a PhD in the late seventies where he met Mum, who was training as a Midwife. They landed good jobs upon their return to Nigeria, Dad as a lecturer in the Zoology Department, and Mum as a nurse at the University Health Centre. As civil servants, they were relatively well paid and commanded the respect of the community.

Mum had heard of a couple who had successfully built a thriving tuition business outside the campus, at the Seventh Day Secondary School in Lagere. Mr Emmanuel and Aunty Helen, as they were known, were teaching probably close to a hundred children every weekday after normal school hours. Having made her enquiries and signed up Wolex and me, she asked a carpenter to quickly make a desk and chair for each of us.

On our first day, although we arrived at the venue on time, we were lumbered with our brand-new desks and chairs. Another student from OAU campus began walking alongside us.

'Would you like me to help you with the chair?' he asked.

'Yes, please'. Wolex jumped at his offer, leaving me to struggle to keep up.

'Those are nice desks. Where did you get them from?'

'Mum's carpenter made them', Wolex replied proudly. 'He's really good'.

'They are different from the desks we use here, *sha*'.

'And why is that?' I asked, hoping that we hadn't made a major blunder that would cause us problems later.

'Well, the ones we use here are made of metal, not wood like yours'.

'But why would anyone decide it's sensible to make their desks and chairs out of metal? They'd be heavy, wouldn't they? And expensive'.

'I guess you'd have to ask the Seventh Day School authorities'.

'Why? What has Seventh Day got to do with your desks?'

'Because we borrow the desks and chairs. The school owns them. Their students have left for the day, so the school is happy for us to borrow them for our tuition. I think Mr Emmanuel made some kind of arrangement with the school. Sometimes, we do find that we are slightly short of desks and chairs, but it's rare. Anyway, why did you guys decide to make your own desks and chairs?'

His question was met with silence. We stopped for a moment. We had reached the entrance to the hall where the tuition was being held. Although we expected the students to look in our direction with curiosity because we were newcomers, the puzzled looks we received showed how out of place we looked, carrying the unnecessary furniture. I desperately wanted the floor to open up and swallow us.

There were no introductions or attempts to ease us into the flow of things. Within a few minutes, the lesson started and the focus shifted very quickly from the newbies who had just joined to the subject being taught that day. Tuition lessons focused mainly on Mathematics, English Language, and Science.

The first observation a newcomer would make was that this tuition outfit was not just another class set-up, like the ones we were used to in our respective primary schools. The discipline was extreme at best, out of control at worst, a teaser of what awaited those of us who would attend boarding schools in later years. Forget Tiger parents: these tuition teachers were like military dictators. They pushed us hard. Although corporal punishment was, and remains, part of student life in Nigeria, at tuition the punishments were worse than anywhere, even our homes. Our parents never complained, or stepped in. If a student's birthday fell on a weekday, the student discouraged his or her parents from throwing a party. Attending tuition became the most important aspect of one's week. If the party went ahead, other students from the tuition group were expected to decline their invitations. If students skipped tuition for a birthday party, they were punished the next day, sometimes severely.

Mr Emmanuel's reach extended far beyond the tuition class, into our primary schools. He appointed some students to enforce his standards when we were at our respective schools during the day. These spies were killjoys. We despised them. He expected us to spend our break times, sometimes lunch hour, in the library, instead of playing football, or having fun, like we were used to. It was painful to see those kids who were not under this subjugation having all the fun. Any time tuition began with Mr Emmanuel wearing a smile on his face as he launched into a speech or a series of questions, we could smell a rat.

'How is everyone? I hope you've had a good day'.

'Yes, sir', the class responded, though not very convincingly.

'I've had a brilliant day. In fact, my day was so brilliant I finished early, around noon. I then decided to see how the people I care about most in life were doing. Guess what I did?'

No response from the class.

'You don't want to know?' he teased. 'I'll tell you anyway. I decided to head over to Staff School. *Sebi*, that's your school,

6

yes?' he said, looking around the class. 'Most of you, anyway?'

His comments triggered some murmurings as the students reflected, trying to remember what their day had been like, and whether there was anything that could be used against them and lead to some kind of punishment.

'Why all the noise?' he demanded. 'Show some respect!'

The class fell silent, immediately.

'As I was saying, I went over to your school to see how you lovely people were doing. Being the model students I thought you were, I went straight to the Library because that's where I knew you'd all be, studying away, since education is the most important thing. That's what you're in school for, isn't it?'

Nobody spoke.

'Isn't it!'

'Yes it is, sir'.

'There were five of you in the Library. A total of five!'

One could have heard a pin drop.

'Dayo, Chinedu, Ife, Tosin, Ekpong – where are you?'

The five stood up. He then launched into a mini lecture, his Igbo accent betraying his origin.

'The rest of you should be ashamed of yasef. You think coming first doesn't come through hard work, *ehn*? You're in school to study, not to play. Life is full of competition. There is more room at the top. If you prefer to stay at the bottom, you'll struggle and struggle and struggle'.

Everyone hoped this would be the end of it.

'As a reward for your behaviour, in addition to your homework for the weekend, you will be sitting a Maths and English comprehension test, first thing on Monday'.

That statement was enough to wreck our weekend and was met with groans from every corner of the class.

7

After completing our assignments, tests, or exams, we marked each other's scripts on the tuition premises. There was nothing unusual about this, except that Mr Emmanuel had devised a system to ensure cheating was made practically impossible. We passed our answer scripts backwards to the next student, not forwards, and then sometimes sideways to make it as difficult as possible to influence, plead, or collude with the marker. Low marks earned students a flogging that would be seared into their memory for months.

The content of the curriculum we were taught was beyond that of our current year, and Mr Emmanuel was obsessed with current affairs quizzes. After our first quiz, Wolex and I shared our thoughts as we walked towards the car park.

'How many did you think you answered correctly?' he asked me.

'Honestly I don't know'.

'But you guessed, right?'

'Some, yeah. First woman to drive in Nigeria? I didn't have a clue'.

'I heard one of the other boys mention it yesterday. It's Fela's mum, Mrs Kuti. I think Mum mentioned that Grandma might be related to their family somehow'.

'Good for you. I guess that info will be useful to me next time. There were too many questions on the coat of arms. The eagle – I guessed it means strength?'

'Yes, that's correct'.

'And the flag – the colours. White. That must be peace. And green? Surely vegetation or the forest?'

'Yes. You probably did better than you thought', Wolex said.

'I hope so'.

Instead of the textbooks we used in school, Mr Emmanuel

utilised a series of Mathematics textbooks by Larcombe. As far as we were concerned, these books contained the most difficult questions known to man. His goal was to ensure that his tutees got the best marks in the common entrance exams. We felt his wrath when, in my year, the student who came first among the University Staff School pupils was not one of his tutees.

To top it all off, we didn't look forward to the holidays, because sometimes our homework list was so long that we had to compare notes to ensure we got every question he had dictated. This was the mother of all homework.

As much as we detested the rigours of tuition, we could see visible improvements in our performance in school. And while tuition combined students across three different school years, there was no hierarchy. No one lorded anything over any other person. It was impossible for a bullying culture to develop under Mr Emmanuel's watch. And even if we had a bad day at tuition, home awaited us every evening, with decent food, the comfort of a bed, and a roof over our heads. Theft was not rife, and responsibilities were limited at home, school, or tuition.

All that was about to change. Boarding school was just around the corner.

Chapter 2

January 8, 1990. It was the start date at Wolex's new secondary school. Although we had grown up on one of the most prestigious university campuses in Nigeria, our parents decided, for reasons we could not understand, to ship him off to boarding school far away from home. In the absence of league tables, they relied on word of mouth and hearsay to decide on their choice of school. Of their many friends, the views of a certain Mrs Tola swayed them the most. She was a fellow nurse with my mum at the Health Centre. Her input was valuable because her home state, Ondo, was the one which Mum and Dad were considering for Wolex.

The previous year, Mum had travelled the length of Ondo State, visiting the reputable schools in the state with Mrs Tola. This was her due diligence tour before sending off her firstborn to a life with strangers. Dad was happy to interrogate and pore over the feedback Mum and Mrs Tola came back with from their travels.

Built into the fabric of the Nigerian system is positive discrimination. This is particularly true of the education system. Cut-off marks for common entrance exams varied, depending on a student's state of origin. The more developed states in the south of the country boasted higher levels of literacy and attainment than those in the north. But on a regional level, there were admission criteria guiding intake numbers, based on the state of origin of the students.

Ile-Ife, the town we grew up in, is in Osun State, which used to be part of Oyo State. Osun State was carved out of Oyo State eighteen months after Wolex started secondary school. The school my parents eventually settled on was situated in Owo, a town in neighbouring Ondo State, one hundred and fifty kilometres, or two hours and thirty minutes by car, from Ile-Ife. Given that our family's home state was Osun, it was not automatic that Wolex would gain admission into Ondo State schools. Somehow, instead of the Owo school which my parents preferred, Wolex ended up on the admission list of a school in Oye-Ekiti, another town in Ondo State. As a result, Mum and Mrs Tola travelled to the Ondo State Ministry of Education to correct what they thought was a simple administrative error. After seven of such trips, they succeeded, but only as far as getting Wolex on the waiting list of the Owo school. So, off to Owo they went. On their return, they debriefed my dad.

'It was a close call. If we had not visited that school, he would not have secured the admission', my mum, relieved, shared with Dad.

Mum and Mrs Tola had requested a meeting with the Principal to make a case for Wolex to be admitted.

'I'm glad to inform you that two places have opened up for admission', the Principal's assistant said.

'That's splendid news', mum exclaimed. 'I hope that means Wolex has a place'.

'Well, it depends on the Principal, ultimately. The waiting list is fifteen strong'.

'Is the Principal around? Can we make a case for Wolex?'

'He went to Akure, but hopefully he should be back today'.

'Are you saying you're not sure if or when he'll be back today?'

'Well, you know, he's the Principal'.

Mum's heart sank. There was no telling when this man would show up. And it was approaching 4:00 p.m. They'd have to leave by 5:00 p.m. to get back to Ile-Ife before it got dark.

'Twenty minutes later, the Principal walks in', Mrs Tola said to my dad.

'What a relief!'

'Yes, it was. We had come so far on this journey, it would have been disappointing to see this admission slip away'.

The Principal greeted them.

'What can I do for you, ladies?'

'Good afternoon, sir. We are here regarding the admission of a student. He passed the—'

'Where's the list?' he interrupted, beckoning to his assistant.

'Here, sir'.

'I already ticked the two names. This one here... and this one too'.

'Sir, this woman's son's name is not one of the two'.

'What's the boy's state of origin?'

Dejectedly, Mum replied, 'Osun, sir, but he scored well in the exam, even though he has a slightly deformed left hand. See, I brought his medical report too'.

'*Ehn*? Put him in a school for the handicapped now. I'm not sure we can help you like that. Where are you from, yourself?'

'Oyo State, sir'.

'So, you don't have any links to Ondo State?'

'No, sir'.

'Sir', Mrs Tola interjected, 'I'm the boy's aunty, and you'll be pleased to know I'm your fellow sister, a true daughter of the soil'.

'Where are you from?'

'Ile Oluji, sir'.

'Ah, you are my true sister. Why didn't you say so earlier? *Haba*! *Oya* PA, please add the boy to the admission list'.

***

Wolex's school was one of nine which Ondo State Government had jurisdiction over. They were called Unity Schools. These were unlike the Federal Government schools, which were amongst the most competitive in the country for admissions. In contrast to Akure, the capital city of Ondo State, where another unity school, St. Peter's, was located, Owo was not as prominent. Of the few reasons my parents preferred Owo, the most significant was potable water. Hellish stories describing students' experiences in relation to water in other boarding schools were enough to push Mum and Dad towards Owo as their preferred choice.

The Owo school was an amalgamation of two teacher training colleges, as the name indicates: St. John and St. Mary. By the late 1980s, the Unity Secondary School tag had been added to reflect a departure from the past college association. Of the few abbreviations that were coined for the name of the school, SAJOMACO proved to be the most popular.

Mum drove Wolex to school that morning of January 8. I was navigator-in-chief, accompanying them on what seemed like a journey into the unknown. Mum loved to drive. She had once driven to and back from Cotonou in neighbouring Benin Republic, a journey of just over six hours, by herself. The journey to Owo felt like an expedition, as we cut through the forest out of Osun State, into Ondo State, with its signature visibly rocky landscape. Mum gave me an interesting task, probably to keep me entertained. I was to note down the names of all the towns and villages we travelled past and record the time it took to travel between each of them. This linear time map became engrained in my subconscious such that, years later, I could wake up during the journey and figure out in less than a minute where exactly we were.

We arrived at SAJOMACO before noon. The campus grounds were bustling with activity – the usual scene on the first day of term. Cars and motorcycles trooped in and out, blaring their horns and kicking up the Harmattan dust. But that didn't bother anyone. New students arrived on campus, confused, not knowing the school grounds well. Parents tried their best to help them settle in, asking teachers and older students questions. Sometimes the parents hopped into Owo town quickly to buy an item the students had forgotten back home.

Wolex's dormitory mates made their introductions and some of the older students provided useful briefings to the newcomers, who stuck out like a sore thumb. Everything about them was new – their clothes, suitcases, metal buckets, kerosene lanterns, water bottles, padlocks, and so on. This contrasted with the seniors, whose uniforms were worn and sometimes shabby. Their demeanour lacked any real spark. The novelty of school life away from home had worn off these older students. The picture I observed in the seniors was the destiny that awaited all newcomers, sometimes nicknamed

Johnny Just Come, or JJC, although it was difficult to entertain that thought at that moment.

Soon, it was time for Mum and me to say our goodbyes. Wolex, being the firstborn in the family, was showing me that he was taking this bold step at such a young age towards maturity. Truth be told, he did not really have any say in the matter. A composed Wolex bid us farewell – no tears. And of course, maturity comes with not missing home, or not showing that one misses home.

Later, Mum and Dad would wrestle with their decision to enrol Wolex at SAJOMACO. By 1990, life was becoming more difficult in Nigeria. Politics featured heavily in family conversations. An attempted military coup in April of that year to overthrow the government of General Babangida made things even worse. The coup was not successful. Reprisals were swift and bloody, and human rights abuses worsened. The tensions were felt more in places like OAU because the universities had been on a collision course with the government for several months before then. Some of the OAU lecturers were very outspoken in their criticism of the government.

'They rounded up Olorode and Awopetu, you know? I just heard', said Dad in a rather subdued voice, peeking through the window as if he suspected someone was listening.

'*Ehn*, really? What is this country turning into? But these are innocent lecturers for God's sake', Mum replied, exasperated.

'They said it is linked to the coup. You know Awopetu is stubborn. God knows what he said or is alleged to have said. Of course, I'm sure he has nothing to do with the coup. This military government – I worry. How can they just link them to it like that?'

15

'It baffles me. I think they are trying to send them a message', Mum said.

'Well, I just pray this country doesn't explode. Did you hear about what they are doing in Lagos, in Maroko? Those poor people'.

'I heard, yes. How can you make three hundred thousand people homeless? Just like that!' she exclaimed, throwing up her arms. Honestly, I don't know where this country is going. Before we know it, the education sector will be in tatters. I just hope and pray that choosing boarding school was the right decision. Maybe we should have considered Moremi more. At least it's on campus and he'd be going from home'.

'But we wanted him to experience life, proper life, outside this place', Dad said. 'Surely, that's a major factor. And you also know the Ondo people, how seriously they take their education'.

'I'm not disagreeing, but those kids who went to Moremi still turned out all right'.

'Let's see how it goes. We can always change schools'.

***

The stories Wolex told us in his first year about boarding school were more exciting than the narrow offerings available on TV. Sometimes Dad would offer to punctuate our boredom at home by suggesting we re-watch one of the seven VHS movies we owned.

'After dinner, would anyone like to watch *The Sound of Music*?' Dad would ask. 'It'd be good to watch something other than *Danger Mouse*, *Matlock*, wrestling, and *Voltron* that you children binge on'.

'Yes! But can we watch *The Wild and the Free* instead?'

'I'll have to clean the tape first. It's getting a bit dusty. Maybe Wolex can tell us another story about boarding school while you wait?'

'Why not? Although this will be a quick one', Wolex replied. 'I don't want Dad to use me as an excuse to send us to bed halfway through the movie'.

'It's OK, Wolex, carry on'.

'OK, so, last term, there was this senior in the third year, called Jide. There were rumours that he liked a girl in the fourth year. Jide is tall for his age, and sometimes people think he is in the senior years. He's also a smooth talker'.

'He must get into trouble because of his size. Do other older students try and bully him?' our younger brother, Yemsta, asked.

'Not necessarily. Sometimes his size is a blessing because some of the other seniors don't realise he's their junior, or maybe because they fear him but won't admit it'.

'Ah, lucky guy'.

'Anyway, there was another boy in the girl's year who also liked her. Somehow, the older boy found out that Jide had been speaking to the girl, and got really angry'.

'Please don't tell me they got into a fight'.

'Be patient now, don't rush ahead of the story', Wolex chastised me. 'So, the senior – I don't know how true this is, but this is what I was told, *sha* – decided to get back at Jide. One day while class was in session, he sneaked back to the dormitory. Jide's room was unlocked. He let himself in and rubbed some dried leaves of *werepe* – what people call the devil's bean plant – onto his towel'.

'I'm already feeling like I need to scratch', Yemsta said.

'There's a twist. That evening, Jide's room head decided to borrow his towel'.

'Nooooo! That's disgusting! I hope you don't allow other people to use your towel', Mum said, recoiling.

'That's your mother', Dad said. 'See how she ignored the *werepe* – as if the boy would die simply because he used another boy's towel. I know it's not hygienic, but the *werepe* is worse'.

'The room head threw the towel around his arm, and, yep, he scratched and scratched. At least when we come into contact with this horrible plant here at home, an adult applies palm oil to soothe the skin'.

'How bad was it?'

'All that scratching made him hysterical'.

'Oh my goodness. Did he find out who had been behind this?' Yemsta asked.

'Yes *o*. The senior must have confided in someone who was very bad at keeping a secret. When the room head discovered this was supposed to have been a prank on Jide, he forced the senior to take off his shirt. He brushed his neck, arms, back and tummy with the *werepe*. By the time the scratching subsided, the senior's body was bloody and covered with lacerations'.

'Did someone report the senior to one of your teachers? I can't believe what I'm hearing'.

'No *o*. Things have to be really bad before we report to teachers. They are not as friendly as you think'.

'What do you mean? You children will always complain that your teachers are strict anyway', Mum said.

'Some of them are *o*, like Mr Fala', Wolex continued.

'Wolex has told us some scary stories about that teacher, Mum', the usually calm Yemsta interjected. 'I think I'll run away if I saw him'.

18

'Is he that man we saw with the Principal, near the gate, on your first day?'

'That was Mr Ologs. We don't mind him. He's not as strict. Mr Fala is easy to recognise because he walks with a funny limp. I'm not sure how he got it'.

'Maybe a car accident? I wouldn't be surprised, given the state of those roads'.

'Nobody knows, but even in the dark, you can tell when he is approaching. My room head and some of the other seniors had warned me and my friends to avoid him like a plague. The man is a disciplinarian'.

'Disciplinarian *ba wo*? You children sha. That was how you complained and complained about Mr Emmanuel? He's this, he's that. *Sebi* you all passed your exams, *abi*? What exactly have you seen this Mr Fala do, or is it *won ni won ni*, all hear say?'

'No *o*. One afternoon, my friend Kehinde was going to bathe just as the rest of us were heading to the dining hall for lunch. He was worried he might not make it to the hall before lunch was over, so he shouted to one of his roommates to help collect his plate. Unfortunately, Mr Fala happened to be near, but Kehinde didn't know'.

'So, he got punished for shouting?' Dad asked.

'No, not that. Mr Fala likes to police the speaking of vernacular on campus. He goes about it like it's a religion. You know how we're only meant to speak English at school, so if he finds anyone speaking Yoruba, Igbo, Hausa or any other local language, he will punish the person'.

'*Ehn*, but I think parents don't mind that. We want you all to speak good English', Mum retorted.

'Yes, Mum, but you know we can't speak English all the time.

19

Kehinde was just unfortunate that day'.

'So, how much trouble did he get himself into?'

'When Mr Fala wants to punish us, he will pinch the flesh under the upper arm for long enough that the pain becomes unbearable, almost cutting off the blood supply in the process'.

Mum and Dad were stunned. 'My God! What kind of school is this?'

Chapter 3

A year after Wolex started at SAJOMACO, it was my turn. Although I had been fortunate to catch up with him in primary school on the back of a double promotion, Mum and Dad insisted I complete all six years of primary school, unlike Wolex, who skipped the final year. His was the route most students took. Our parents held me back because they felt the rush was unnecessary, and to give Wolex some breathing space.

I was extremely excited to embark on this adventure, even if temporarily. By this time, Mum had been away from home in London, working, for close to three months. She made the case to Dad that it was a risk worth taking to travel to London and work for a few months to offset the deterioration in living standards we were experiencing because of Nigeria's economic challenges. Nurses were in high demand, even as far away as Saudi Arabia.

A few of my OAU primary school classmates had also secured admission to SAJOMACO. Most of them originated from Ondo State, like Tee. His mum, Mrs Nadet, had more up-to-date information regarding the on-goings in the state than my parents. The morning of the day we were to start school, Mrs Nadet arrived at our house.

'Good morning. Hope you're all well today?' she greeted us, as she walked towards the house.

'All is well. The day has finally arrived for this lot to be sent off', my dad replied gleefully.

'Well, maybe not so fast, sir', Mrs Nadet said.

'Why? Is there an update from the school, a delay of some sort?'

'Yes, the government has postponed the start date till later in the month for new students. That's the news we picked up early this morning'.

'Really? That's unfortunate. What is the reason behind the postponement?'

By this time, I had emotionally checked out of the conversation. After all the excitement and the adrenaline rush, now this, I thought, feeling deflated. My suitcase was packed, along with the million or so items the school had asked us to bring along. I would have to unpack everything. It was an abrupt and premature end to a day that had started so well. Dad ended up driving Wolex to SAJOMACO since the delay didn't affect the other students, leaving a despondent me behind to ponder what could have led to this disaster of a situation. It would be weeks before I would see Wolex and begin my adventure in boarding school.

The start date was postponed at least one more time before I eventually headed to school on February 28, 1991. Mrs Nadet was the bearer of the bad news each time. The seven weeks I spent waiting at home remain the most boring in my life to date. In the weeks that followed the initial postponement, apart from a few students who were also affected by the Ondo State delay, the rest of my friends on the university campus began secondary school as expected; some left home for boarding school in other states. Even my younger siblings, Yemsta and Nasa, would disappear from 8:00 a.m. to 2:00 p.m. for school, and then later in the afternoon for after-school tuition. Although dad would pop back home briefly for lunch, he was lecturing at the university most of the day. In the meantime, I had my seventy-year-old grandmother for company. Overcoming the inevitable boredom caused by the sixty-year gap between us was impossible.

While it felt like millennia had passed, February 28 did eventually come. It was with some trepidation that we welcomed Mrs Nadet into our house that morning. Although she informed us that she wasn't aware of any further post-ponement, this did not equate to a guarantee that all was well. Notwithstanding, that was good enough for me.

The journey to Owo felt shorter this time around. By now, given my previous visits to see Wolex during visiting days, I was no stranger to some parts of the boys' dormitory. There were four houses – Akinyele, Lennon, Okusanya and Vining. I was put in Akinyele, away from Wolex's Vining. It didn't bother me that we were in different houses because I was raring for my secondary school days to begin. I barely recollect waving goodbye to Dad. His car turned right outside the school gate and disappeared, as he sped towards the motorway.

'Finally, freedom at last', I muttered.

***

Somehow, waking up at 5:00 a.m. the following day was easier for me than 6:30 a.m. for family devotions back at home. The excitement of this adventure was still very palpable. March 1 was Founders' Day – a reference to the date the school was established. Every year, students – boys and girls – participate in a light procession, marching out of the school grounds through a defined route in Owo town, back into the school, finally ending up on the playing fields next to the school chapel. At the end of the procession, the students sang the school anthem.

To the praise, honour and glory
  Of our dear, great benefactor
  We raise our beautiful anthem
  To laud the land of true knowledge
  Raise the anthem
  Ye old students
  To be echoed by the present
  We will sing the glory of our dear benefactor
  Saint John Mary's

Along with the other new students, I did my best to mumble along, but raised my voice with confidence once I recognised a section I had picked up from Wolex in the past.

Although we all made it back to the school grounds safely, one of my OAU friends, Rex, had a slight mishap. The sole of one of his Cortina shoes came off completely during the long walk back. The brand-new shoe was not fit for purpose, a sign of things to come, as we soon discovered we had become victims of substandard and counterfeit products, which were spreading across Nigeria. I did not allow Rex's bad news to alter my mood, or to make me consider the prospect of missing my parents or home. There was more to explore and enjoy.

Given that March 1 was a Friday, everyone was keen for the weekend to begin. Our classrooms were not ready, so we spent the day relaxing. By late afternoon, many of the first-year students ended up wandering around the school grounds, still exploring. Some found their way into the music storage room. This so-called room was a non-descript building situated between Akinyele House, the administrative office building and the Principal's house. Bizarrely, it sat right in the middle of a farm. I suspect the farm came later, but these were not the thoughts that preoccupied the mind of a ten-year-old at the time. Many of the musical instruments that were kept in the store were prehistoric, and gathering dust. Some were damaged with no hope of ever being repaired. So, they were left to rot away. By the time I left SAJOMACO, I looked back to those early days and was grateful for the fact that, at least in 1991, we had a variety of musical instruments to speak of.

The students who made their way into this music storage building were mostly naive first-year students. They were not aware that they were trespassing, literally. Unfortunately, Mr Fado, our music teacher, got wind of what the students were up to. He made his way swiftly to the building and decided his best option for punishing them was to lock the entire lot inside and walk away. In classic Nigerian parenting style, 'teaching them a lesson' took precedence over safety or security.

Word soon reached Akinyele House that a teacher had locked up some students in the music storeroom. Along with other busybodies, I made my way to the building, but did not get too close for fear of getting myself into trouble. This episode lasted for at least thirty minutes while we stood and watched, helpless. The students' faces were pressed against the thick burglary proofing which crisscrossed the window. It occurred to me that I could have been one of them. The fear on their faces was gripping. The episode was a rude awakening

25

to the fact that SAJOMACO had rules of engagement that new students were oblivious to. If this was a punishable offence, what exactly was the offence, and how severe was the punishment likely to be? Worse still, there were no parents to appeal to.

Thankfully, luck was on the students' side that evening. They only got a telling off from Mr Fado. But the impression that school was a cocoon-like Eden was being shattered – and only on our second day. Maybe home was not so terrible after all.

Term soon got underway and we were buried in schoolwork over the next four weeks. Juggling classwork and assignments with the harsh realities of living with other students, especially our seniors, was a learning process for all of us.

*****

A point comes in the life of a first-year student when he or she starts to reminisce about home. The trigger is random. It varies from student to student and can be as mundane as the sudden realisation that SAJOMACO will be one's reality for six long years. For others, it was more serious – bullying and maltreatment were a certainty. The only question was timing.

One of the more serious incidences – especially the first time it happens – involved losing one's keys. Padlocks and keys were necessities of life in school, for the lockers and suitcases that housed our food items, shoes, clothes, and so on. Losing the keys spelt the onset of a miserable period. It was not unusual to hear stories of first-year students who had misplaced their master keys, and having kept the duplicates inside their lockers, had no obvious way of retrieving the latter.

Others absentmindedly left the master key in their lockers, alongside the duplicate, and closed the padlock.

Tee and Bykes were my closest friends. Bykes was also from OAU. The three of us had been members of a renowned children's choir at the university. A couple of weeks after we started at SAJOMACO, we decided we had spent enough time away from home to warrant writing letters to our families. We had not heard from any family member, directly or indirectly, for weeks. Although there was a telephone in the Principal's office, students were only permitted to use it when there was an emergency. And we had not received any letters. Our parents believed in keeping their distance, and so did we.

Stamped envelopes which doubled as writing paper were common and the preferred choice at the time. In 1991, our school had its own post office. A shadow of this post office remained when I left SAJOMACO for good.

The three of us started to write our letters. It was the first time we would take time out to think about our families properly. Reflecting over the experiences we had had in those weeks at school was overwhelming. For Tee, it proved too much.

'Tee. Tee. Tee! Are you sniffling? Are you crying?'

'Of course I'm not', he replied, looking away from me and using his forearm to wipe his face.

'He is crying, you know, Bunmi', Bykes chuckled. 'Ha, ha, ha, I never thought I'd see the day. Strong Tee, I guess boarding school does take its toll'.

'Tee. You know you're a big boy now', I said with a grin. 'So, you are jelly on the inside too?'

Tee's eyes dried soon after. It was as though he needed to get through this moment, like it was some sort of rite of passage.

To Bykes and me, Tee was weak – he cried because he missed his family. To us, boarding school was supposed to be about leaving home for weeks and maturing. As far as we were concerned, what happened to Tee was not going to happen to us, especially having seen Tee crumble and let his emotions get the better of him. What did we know?

End of term arrived. The reunion with our parents was worth the wait. All the emotions we had held back could flow, but these were still smiles and laughter. However, there was a small twist, one which we were aware of, but did not fully appreciate its ramifications.

In 1991, the academic year changed in Nigeria from January–December to September–August. Given that the start to our first year was delayed by two months effectively, this meant that our entire first year was crammed into a March–July period. As a result, our Easter holiday felt more like a half-term break, and before we knew it, we were back in school. But this time, the most senior students in the sixth year were in school with us. Given that their final year exams were only a couple of months away, the school asked them to return early for extra revision classes.

Blending in was easier when hundreds of boys were around. With just the first and sixth-year students on campus, there was nowhere to hide. Thankfully, because the gap in age was wide, the sixth-year students were kinder to us than any other year would have been. It was also easier to respect these 'grown men', as they seemed to us at the time.

From our return after the Easter break till the end of the academic year, it was a total of sixteen weeks. The length sent shivers down one's spine. During this period, we did see our families on visiting days, the first Saturday of every month, but those sixteen weeks felt like sixteen years. It was traumatic at times knowing that we were not going to leave the school grounds the entire time. We were in prison. It was common to find the chalkboard in different classrooms with inscriptions like '10 weeks and 4 days to go' as we counted down the days. Even if the busyness of life distracted us, occasionally an incident occurred which exposed our frailties, how raw our emotions were as well as our deep longing for home.

My 'Tee moment' came shortly after we returned from the short Easter break. It was a Saturday. I had been hanging out with Tee and Bykes at the chapel, practising some songs. As we made our way back to the dormitory, the Chaplain's daughter delivered a message to both of them that her father, their guardian, needed their help on his small farm. My guardian was another teacher who was transitioning out of the school at the time. As such, I rarely saw him.

So, off the two went, leaving me on my own. All the grandstanding I had projected of a tough and mature eleven-year-old crumbled. The isolation was painful. I retreated to my room and reflected on my life. I felt like the kid remaining in the circle whom nobody had picked to play with. Like Tee, I thought about my family and desperately wished my brother Wolex was with me. The tears ran, and I turned into a blubbering mess.

My melancholy was interrupted by a loud bang on the door.

'Recker! Recker!' shouted someone on the other side of the door.

It had to be a sixth-year student for the person to call Senior Recker by name. He acquired the name because he was a human termite, notorious for always carrying on his person

29

a spoon which was capable of lifting half of the contents of a plate of food.

To save face, I quickly wiped my eyes, pulled myself together, and opened the door.

There was no one there. I looked up and down the hallway. It was deserted.

I didn't cry after that interruption. I had gotten it out of my system. However, after that, I became sympathetic to those who missed home.

Chapter 4

B y the final term of our first year, we had settled well into life at SAJOMACO, but occasionally, a random event happened that reminded us that the world we were in was far from normal. Bykes, Tee and I hung out in each other's rooms for long enough that our respective roommates – the seniors – got to know us well. Jetta, who was in Vining House with Tee, occasionally joined us since he was my classmate. Late one evening, my room head, Senior Steevo, who was also the Akinyele House Captain, summoned the other six occupants of Room 1 for a meeting.

'Something serious happened today', he began. 'But I'm determined to get to the bottom of it'.

This was the first time I'd see him with such a serious face. He meant business.

'I kept some money in my locker last night. When I checked for it this evening, it had disappeared. Clearly, someone knew about the money and stole it while I was out'.

Theft of buckets of water, or even food, occurred occasionally. Students learned to live with it. But theft of money was a serious offence, irrespective of the amount.

'Senior Steevo, you know I was out all day today', one of the seniors said.

'*Walai*, it wasn't me', another one added.

'I'm not accusing anybody. I have a plan', Senior Steevo carried on. 'I want a list of everybody that came into this room today. *Shey* you hear me?'

'Yes, Senior Steevo'.

'Don't miss anybody out. And you Bunmi, that includes all your friends', he added, pointing at me.

So, someone was dispatched to round up my friends from their respective dormitories. When they arrived, Senior Steevo was in full flow with his interrogation, one person at a time. The rest of us were outside, waiting for our turn to be called in. The process carried on for almost thirty minutes. Bykes was the last person to be called in. When he entered, we were also in the room, having coughed up whichever names we could remember.

'Who came into this room while you were here earlier today?'

Bykes stood still, almost drowning in his oversized house wear, his eyes darting across from one person to another.

'The only person I remember is Senior Roberts', he said, sheepishly.

'You're sure? No one else?'

'I'm sure Senior Steevo'.

'Do any of you remember Senior Roberts being here?' Senior Steevo turned to Tee, Jetta and me.

We all shook our heads.

Senior Steevo left the room shortly after to seek out each student on his list.

After that, we left the room to hang out in Room 2 with another friend. After about thirty minutes, someone violently swung open the door.

'Which of you is Bykes?'

Every head turned towards the far corner of the room where my friend was perched on the edge of a bunk bed.

'They said you said I stole money'.

'No *o*, Senior Roberts. Senior Steevo asked us…' Bykes lifted himself off the bed, hoping to finish the sentence. Standing up, he carried on. 'He asked us if we remembered…'

Wham!

The slap cut him short.

'And you said you didn't say I stole the money. But you open your mouth now and said it was me. You gave him my name, *abi?*'

Bykes, staggering backwards, buried his face in his palms, partly defending himself from any follow-up slap, partly nursing the pain. He must have been seeing stars. It was a sobering sight – to see how much power a fourteen-year old could wield over someone who was only three years younger. He eventually came to, sat quietly for about fifteen seconds while Senior Roberts carried on shouting at him. Suddenly, he jumped off the bed like a possessed animal.

'You bully! I told you Senior Steevo asked me a question. All I did was tell him you had come to the room like other people! Is it a crime to answer a question? You can't just slap me like that! What are you going to do? Slap me again?'

When a SAJOMACO junior student gives a senior a piece of his mind publicly like Bykes did, he is said to have 'raked for' the senior.

Bykes was done. Whatever spirit had possessed him left as quickly as it came. He retreated and gently sat down on the bed, with a puzzled but relieved look. It was as if he didn't believe what he had just done. This was not the Bykes we knew.

And students with a diminutive stature like his certainly were not known to take the fight to our seniors like he did.

Senior Roberts was so shocked that he left the room without saying a word. He never came near Bykes again. And my friend also did his best to avoid him. Bykes' stature drew a lot of sympathisers his way. Some just adored him and made themselves his de facto big brother. So, when they heard of Senior Roberts' antics, they gave him a piece of their mind and did their best to protect Bykes for the rest of their time at the school. As for the thief, let's just say he lived to steal another day.

***

Despite the erosion of standards and a poor maintenance culture in the country, OAU grounds evoked a beauty that was unmatched in Nigeria. The roads were tarred and well maintained; electricity was supplied via underground cables in contrast to the messy spaghetti-like overhead cable structures that were the norm outside the university grounds; the grass was tended to, with beautiful lawns and flowers adorning the landscape. There was a zoo and a museum, a grand auditorium named after Oduduwa, who is said to have been the first ruler of Ile-Ife, an amphitheatre, a hospital complex, a commercial farm, botanical gardens, and more.

What I swapped OAU for in SAJOMACO was closer to the real Nigeria. And that meant some lessons had to be learnt the hard way. For starters, there was a major adjustment in terms of the power supply. We used kerosene lanterns a lot more at SAJOMACO than back at home because of severe power shortages, more so in the later years as Nigeria fell into disarray. The wick of a kerosene lantern is designed to burn slowly, with a mechanism enclosed within the glass casing, directly above the fuel tank, in which the wick is suspended. The design ensures the wick is slowly released upwards as the flame burns. The ideal lantern burns at a constant rate once the length of the wick is set at the desired height by a rotating handle.

While the lanterns at home were generally made to a high standard, most of those I saw at SAJOMACO were of inferior quality, from the metal casing to the wick and even the kerosene. The worst lanterns were a major fire hazard. Learning to dismantle or clean them was relatively straightforward – except for novices like me – because 'Aunty' Victoria, our house help, would have sorted things out. A few of us ended up with serious burns. Others cracked the glass casing because they dipped it in water while it was still hot.

The initial weeks spent at SAJOMACO were a shock to the system. There were no tarred roads anywhere on campus, so dust became a part of life. Most of the buildings that served as dormitories were built with mud or clay, and later plastered with cement on the exterior. None of the windows had mosquito netting.

As a result of the dust, asthma sufferers had to find a way to cope. Forgetting to bring their inhalers was equivalent to a death wish. Thankfully, the school authorities had enough sense to exempt these students from manual labour as long as they had a medical note from a doctor, which they could not afford to lose. There was no centralised view on what these students were exempt from, in terms of school duties. No one could blame a student for pushing the boundaries by seeking exemptions from almost every task. A hot-headed teacher might push back but, for the most part, the exemption letters proved too powerful to ignore. Senior students defied these exemptions more, however. This was because they had a much longer menu of tasks they could ask the juniors to perform. Given that exemption letters were primarily aimed at manual labour, such as gardening and agricultural work, senior students felt that the washing of plates, running errands, and fetching of water did not qualify. For the sake of peace, junior students tended to capitulate to the seniors' demands.

Our dormitories did not have bathrooms or lavatories near them. This was probably deliberate, for health and safety reasons. However, I struggled to adjust to the bathing experience for two reasons.

First, I had to acclimatise to the cold water. How I missed the Ariston water heater back home! When water was scarce, rainwater was a necessary substitute. Practical experience with rainwater at SAJOMACO taught us the difference between hard and soft water, the latter having a soapy feel.

Second, for someone who had grown up in a nuclear household, a communal bathing experience was very strange to me. Being stark naked in front of other students was unsettling. Worse still, some of these students – the older teenagers who were in the fifth and sixth years – were men in my eyes. I could not believe the size of their manhood, and how much pubic hair was on display. The learning curve on puberty was like a baptism of fire, because it was right there in my face, and nobody had prepared me for it.

And the lavatories. What lavatories? These were pit latrines. They were a cesspit of vermin, because the attention they were given was inadequate. There were some toilets around the dormitories, but those dated back to the teacher training college days of SAJOMACO. What was left were relics: abandoned rooms that had decayed into a sorry state. The latrines were our modern-day toilets. As squeamish as we may have felt initially, the call of nature was too strong. Students came to school armed with toilet paper, but it rarely lasted the entire term. A student did not need to be told that any type of paper was a suitable substitute.

The latrines may have been situated away from our dormitories but that was a minor risk we faced hygiene-wise. Boarding school was the equivalent of getting a shot of antibodies because of the constant exposure to germs and pathogens. Mosquitoes were the most common of these. Back at OAU, our windows were covered with nets. At SAJOMACO, they were bare. Consequently, attaching mosquito nets to our bunk beds was a necessity. Still, even though we tried our best to use the nets properly, it was difficult to prevent malaria, because we were exposed to mosquitoes all around the school grounds.

Our clinic was kitted out for basic health needs, but empathy was a word that was lacking in the nurses' dictionary. We regularly battled with a long list of diseases including chicken pox, jaundice, scabies and malaria. Of these, malaria was by far in a league of its own and posed the greatest threat. Yet, we constantly underestimated it. The thought of visiting the clinic for treatment filled one with trepidation such that one would rather hold out to be treated at home if, say, end of term was less than two weeks away. We often wondered why chloroquine, though effective in treating malaria, tasted like the most bitter medicine known to man. Injections were a lifesaver in this respect, but if any student was terrified of needles the clinic certainly did not get the memo. And some of us experienced a horrible side effect of the drug for the first time on campus – away from home: the almighty itch that is worse than a combination of soldier ant bites and pins and needles. My first forty-eight hours reacting to chloroquine was pure, unabating torture.

Even when we appeared healthy, water shone a spotlight on our hygiene deficiency. Although the chlorinated water supplied to the school was fit for drinking, over time, we were forced to experiment with stagnant water held in large reservoir tanks. Even a fool knew the water was far from hygienic. That said, for bathing purposes, we were less fussy. Options for purifying the water were limited. If a snake oil salesman had tried to sell us chalk as a purifier, we would no doubt have tried our luck.

Aluminium sulphate, or alum, became a necessity on the list of items we took to school, along with salt, sugar, and other provisions. Although it precipitates the impurities in water, it is not a disinfectant. So, while the water looked clear and pure, it was still not fit to drink. But we drank the water regardless, tolerating the hint – or nuisance – of sweetness introduced by the alum.

Our brazen approach to drinking partly purified water led boils to spring up all over our bodies. The experience of the older seniors taught us that our antibodies would kick into overdrive and boost our immunity, culminating in the eventual clearing up of the boils. If only Mum realised that our new normal in school – as far as water was concerned – was far removed from the assumptions she and Dad had before SAJOMACO became part of our lives, I thought.

More than anyone else, I missed Mum the most in those early years. Her three-month stay in London turned into eighteen months. In mid-1992, Wolex sat his third-year state-wide exams. He was half-way through his SAJOMACO experience. Once the third-year students finished their exams, they were released early, so Wolex left for home, leaving me behind. On the last day of term, I looked for Dad's car tirelessly, but it was nowhere to be seen. Eventually, I spotted the brown Volkswagen Passat from a long way off. But what I could make out of the profile of the driver didn't fit that of my dad.

'Mum!'

I ran, and once I reached the car, I gave her the biggest embrace I could muster. Onlookers probably thought I was a mummy's boy. If only they knew the backstory. I wished I could brag about her, and her travels, to my friends. But they would care very little about that on the day they were being released from SAJOMACO.

A year later, after my third-year exams, I left for home, leaving Wolex, now in his fourth year, behind at school. It was Rex's mum who picked him, Bykes, and me up. We stopped during the journey to buy Suya, Nigeria's authentic smoked barbecued meat. It was the best way to end junior secondary school.

As the years rolled by, I came to accept SAJOMACO as my second home. I was resigned to my fate, because I knew I was destined to be stuck there for half a decade. That resignation made it slightly more tolerable.

However, it did not mean that I was not petrified when the end of the holidays loomed. Given that the journey from Ile-Ife to Owo took almost three hours, one would assume this was long enough to overcome the anxiety that would have built up as resumption day approached. Quite the opposite. The closer I got to Owo, the more nervous I became. This nervousness dissipated within the first hour of arriving, once

I settled back into school life.

As I moved through the years, my anxiety levels reduced. By the fifth year, it was almost undetectable because I was soon to become one of the kings of the campus. The sixth year ushered in one's top-dog status – the year we became the ultimate seniors. At that point, I even looked forward to leaving home for boarding school. Only then could I truly say I did not miss home any longer.

Chapter 5

O ne of the first things that surprised me at SAJOMACO was how cuisines differed from state to state, even for people who spoke the same language. Some of the more exotic options included grasshoppers, frogs, snakes, wild monkeys, goat's head, and dogs.

While I was never tempted to try any of these, a few years later I found myself regularly sampling unripe fruits and roasted termites.

Beyond food, I also observed that dialects varied significantly. SAJOMACO made me realise that the environment I had grown up in had cocooned me.

I was aware of some variations in my own language, Yoruba, since Dad's Ijesha dialect was different from the Oyo dialect that Mum spoke. What I wasn't prepared for, however, was the Owo dialect, which was barely comprehensible to me. As far as I was concerned, their Yoruba might as well have been classified as a separate language. Years later, I would also learn that hundreds of languages were spoken in Nigeria, not just a handful, as I had initially thought.

The Lagosians deserve a special mention on dialect because they were an interesting revelation to me. Not only did they break basic grammar and pronunciation rules on Yoruba language; they were also the most comfortable with pidgin or broken English.

My Yoruba was the equivalent of Received Pronunciation in English Language. It was stripped entirely of dialect. I found it easier to learn Yoruba as a subject in class because the version taught was the same as what I spoke at home with my siblings. For the Lagosians and many others, our Yoruba classes felt like a rewiring.

Emmanuel was a Lagosian in my year. A short conversation about food betrayed his origins.

'Hey, what's up? Is something wrong?' I asked.

'*Moo tii jeun jare*', he replied. He hadn't eaten.

'You mean *Mi o tii jeun, abi*?' I corrected.

'But what was wrong with what I said?'

'It's not *Moo*, its *Mi o*', I slowly pointed out the difference, even if it was a subtle one. 'You don't join the two words up, and there's nothing like *moo* in the Yoruba language'.

'You Ile-Ife people. We know you're from the cradle of civilisation, but language evolves, you know?'

'That's just a lame excuse. You guys are just a little lazy and you don't recognise it. I'm curious. How would you say "I have eaten"?'

Hesitantly, he replied, '*Mi ti jeun*'.

'Goodness, you guys do turn the language upside down. The *mi* should be *mo*, as in "*Mo ti jeun*"'.

'I hope they won't be this harsh in our Yoruba language class', he said, with a frown.

Most Lagosians, like Emmanuel, were easy to pick out from the crowd, not just because of how they spoke but also because they carried themselves around with the greatest swagger the world had ever seen. I guess it was the city versus town thing.

Many of them just couldn't help showing off. I wondered why any parent would send their children all the way from Lagos to a sleepy backwater town like Owo.

'How come your parents picked Owo? It's a bit further out coming from Lagos than for most people'.

'How long is it from Ile-Ife?'

'Two and a half hours, maybe three', I said.

'Well, from Lagos, it can be six. We go through Ore, then Ondo town'.

'And there was me thinking my journey was long. So why Owo then?'

'Our family are originally from Owo. My grandparents still live here, so it was easy for my parents to pick Owo'.

'Lucky you. At least, you have some family close by. They must send you top-up provisions from time to time'.

'Oh yes, I'm not complaining about that at all', he said with a smile, 'but what I'm not so keen on is the dullness of Owo compared with Lagos'.

'You mean the quiet nature?'

'Everything. It's too quiet'.

'You miss the glitz and glamour'.

'Absolutely. But my parents insist it will help me focus on my studies'.

'I guess they have a point'.

Despite the bravado of Lagosian kids, some of them were dirt poor. But that did not deter them from bragging about life back in Lagos. To them, this Owo experience was a step down. Only after quizzing them properly did we realise that their entire homes could fit into just one room in ours.

The well-to-do Lagosians, on the other hand, were breath-takingly rich. The world I came from was that of modest incomes. To these children, I was little more than a church mouse. Our boarding school set-up was designed to level out the playing field, beginning with our school uniforms. There was no preferential treatment in the allocation of rooms, desks, chairs, and so on. What differentiated the rich students was their pocket money, which the school authorities had no control over.

In my first year, 30 naira was the sum total of my pocket money per term, equivalent to just under five US dollars at the time. It was enough to buy a month's worth of food, assuming two basic meals per day, whereas the poorest of the rich kids could barely survive on 100 naira per term. Thanks to inflation, in my final year my pocket money had risen to 120 naira, while the poorest rich kids struggled to make their 700 naira go the distance. Frugality was a necessity for me. Ironically, at the end of term, I usually had leftover cash. In contrast, the rich kids were more likely to turn to those like me for loans.

Some students experienced a demotion in their status during our boarding school years. The loss of the breadwinner in a family or a parent losing a job or a lucrative contract resulted in a significant cut to pocket monies. Sometimes the trend went the other way. In some instances, we saw upgrades to family cars when the next visiting day came along, or an official car with all the bells and whistles, complete with a driver, especially if it were connected to a government role or a political appointment.

Visiting days were sacrosanct. Having not seen our families for a whole month, we expected them to turn up on that first Saturday of the month bearing goodies. Since my mum was usually abroad, the duty fell on my dad to deliver. He did relatively well in the first few years. But soon, I started to wake up to the fact that there was nothing sacred about these visiting days. Parents started to play fast and loose with this most precious of Saturdays, as the Nigerian economy deteriorated. The value of the naira to the US dollar fell by over 50% during my first three years at SAJOMACO, or by 75% in the parallel market. By 1996, when I left the school, the naira had lost 90% in the parallel market.

The first sign that visiting days were not fail-proof came in the form of carpooling. This made economic sense. Instead of two families driving separate vehicles for hours to SAJOMACO, they could save on fuel expenditure by sharing one car. That was fair enough; we could live with that. Soon, however, the parents extended this efficiency habit to sending our food provisions through other students' parents instead of coming along on the journey.

Up until my fourth year, apart from carpooling, our visiting days were normal. If term was to end in the second week of the month, it was a miracle if the parents showed up on the visiting day, the week prior, for that month. Still, we hoped. On the rare occasion, Dad did not show up because he forgot completely. He would then make up for this howler with a mid-week visit.

My final year was the worst. It coincided with my sister Nasa starting secondary school. Nasa's school, Command Secondary School, was located in Ibadan, Oyo State. Not only were the visiting days for both our schools the same, but Ibadan was in the opposite direction to Owo from Ile-Ife. Visiting both schools on the same day was a herculean task, if not an impossible one. As a result, Dad was forced to pick one school over the other. Nasa was prioritised. Yemsta, who by then had joined me at SAJOMACO, and I were expected to be the understanding, mature, older brothers. We resigned ourselves to the fact that we were now second class on this issue. From that moment on, we were grateful if anything arrived through another parent.

On one of the visiting days in my second year, a brand-new Peugeot 504 pulled up outside my dormitory. Its arrival drew the attention of the entire dormitory. No one knew who the important passenger or owner of the car was, because of the tinted windows. All eyes were on the rear door – the one on the right, next to the owner's corner, as Nigerians are fond of saying, because that is where a VIP would sit. The door opened and out stepped a lady.

'TJ, it's your mum!' Wolex exclaimed, pulling his friend's shirt and dragging him off his bed.

'But that's not our car'.

'But that's your mum, isn't it?'

It was TJ's mum. The state government had just awarded his dad – we never met him throughout our time at SAJOMACO – a brand-new car, as evidenced by the special registration plate. This was 1993. Nigeria was struggling to transition to a democratic government after the military government had refused to honour the results of the elections. TJ's dad must have been doing something right in the eyes of the powers that be.

Although the Peugeot dazzled everyone, it was Rex's dad's car upgrade to a Nissan Pathfinder that became the talk of the campus. This was the Maybach of the time. Rex's dad was juggling a special adviser role to the Federal Government, along with his academic position at OAU. This two-timing between academia and government was enough to make him enemies, but the Pathfinder took the combination of envy, respect, and gossip amongst SAJOMACO students into the stratosphere.

Before my sister Nasa turned our visiting day arrangement upside down, one such day Dad arrived at SAJOMACO with Celia, a lecturer from Trinity College, Dublin, who had travelled to Nigeria to carry out some field work with him. White faces were not unusual in Lagos, or even on the university campus in Ile-Ife. In Owo, however, they were a bit rare.

Celia wanted to see more of the region, so she had tagged along that day. She brought with her a pack of chocolates, including Twix and Wispa. What more could make a hungry, undernourished student happier?

Word spread quickly on campus about Celia – and the ridiculous with it too. Dad had parked in front of Okusanya House, because a tree provided some shade.

'Did you see the *Oyinbo* in front of Okusanya House?' someone said.

'Yes *o*, the one that came with Bunmi's dad'.

'*Ehn, ehn*, I've always wondered where he got his curly hair from. Maybe he's half-caste or something'.

'Half-caste *ke*? That can't be. He's not light-skinned enough'.

'I'm sure he is. Haven't you noticed his unusually long eyelashes?'

This nonsense talk was typical on campus. It didn't help that my mum had travelled to London a few months before I started at SAJOMACO, and she hadn't returned at the time when Celia visited. Explanations as to why India was absent from global football competitions to the nuts and bolts behind the Gulf War came from whoever had the biggest mouth or could pull off an unimaginable story. At times, this was a case of the blind educating the blind, sometimes with a dose of superstition injected.

Claims and counterclaims were a signature of normal everyday chatter, regardless of how ridiculous they got, and the conversations usually descended into loud arguments. By the time a discussion had run its course, we would have shared very little tangible knowledge amongst ourselves. In its place were half-truths or completely wrong information. The devil finds work for idle hands, they say. Something had to fill the ample spare time we were blessed with at school.

Chapter 6

Superstition is embedded in the Nigerian culture. It fuelled the flames of many of the conversations we had on campus. However, beyond the conversations and arguments, there were other forms of it that I was unprepared for, in particular the part it played in a lie-detector test whenever a serious crime was committed, such as the theft of a valuable item. The proponents of this test swore by it, even though these were teenagers. The test materials involved a copy of the Bible, a key, and a string or short rope. It was claimed that if the key was left to dangle on the string, which was placed in the middle of the Bible, as names of students were read out aloud, the key would turn gradually and settle down, facing the culprit.

I never actually witnessed one of these truth-finding sessions, but the fear that gripped a student dormitory when one was in progress was palpable. The impression I got was that the results were mixed, but the legend carried on throughout my secondary school days. Some friendships were damaged irreparably because an innocent party was subjected to this test.

Beyond truth detection, superstition also featured heavily during discussions about the weather, especially rains. It was said that there were some mediums in Owo town who, with their supernatural powers, could control the rains – or, to be more precise, *hold* the rains – while an important event was in progress. Typically, these claims surfaced during crucial football matches which our school was involved in, or very important events in Owo town. No one could really explain why the efficacy of these mediums was statistically insignificant.

Aside from rains, it was also said that there were other mediums who could bring retribution to those who had caused harm to others by throwing a potion or an object at their shadows. There were also exorcisms. This was more of a feature in the girls' dormitories. Almost every year, there would be an incident involving a girl confessing she was a witch. The exorcisms were complete with hysterical behaviour, shouting, screaming, and fainting by the subject in question. It was difficult to tell how much of what was being reported was an act and how much wasn't.

Being a mixed school, boys and girls interacted regularly, but puberty made life complicated. Relationships were forbidden, so any festering crush anyone had on another student was suppressed or met with denial, even if blatantly obvious. Several years after we left SAJOMACO, during a conversation with one of my classmates, she admitted that she had been infatuated with a boy.

'I can tell you this now', she said to me. 'I fancied Baba'.

'No, you didn't!'

'Bunmi, do you know how much of an emotional roller-coaster that was? It was painful. He was in my class, if you remember'.

'Yes, I do. That must have been tough'.

'You can't even begin to imagine. I prayed and prayed that God would take away this feeling, but the more I prayed, the more I fell in love with him!'

'I feel for you. Did you talk about it to anyone?'

She laughed. 'Did I? Why would I? You've forgotten your SAJOMACO? Word would spread. No one could keep a secret. Oh, the pain, the pain!' She flinched, as if in physical pain.

'So, how did you cope?'

'It was dreadful. I couldn't concentrate. Coming to class was like scaling Everest. I was petrified'.

'Did it affect your grades?'

'I don't know. Maybe it did. I always desperately hoped I wouldn't see him whenever I made my way to class. And then, as I approached, right there in front of me he was – gorgeous Baba. I wished a sinkhole would open up beneath me. I couldn't look him in the eye, talk less of uttering a word. Oh Bunmi, it was embarrassing'.

'Did he know?'

'I don't know. Honestly, I don't know'.

'Goodness, you must have suffered. And he was a Muslim, you a Christian. You really were in a bit of a bind'.

'You hit the nail on the head. As if my life wasn't complicated enough already'.

Even though the school authorities strongly discouraged students from engaging in any serious relationships, we had a lot more freedom than we were used to at home. Students responded to this freedom differently. Some exhibited a sense of maturity, while others could be downright reckless. At the mundane end, this freedom was visible in hairstyles we wore and our fashion sense. Peer pressure tested our will daily. The older boys were keen to press their clothes with irons to impress the girls, while for the younger students this issue had not made it onto their priority list yet. At the more serious end, the responsibility to take our education seriously lay in our hands. Making the most of the time designated for prep, for example, was really down to each student.

One important aspect of our lives where school provided an opportunity to break away from home tradition was faith. Apart from Sundays – church service was compulsory, except for Muslims – we weren't accountable to anyone any longer, as far as our individual beliefs were concerned. The school authorities did not impose any demands on us in terms of participation in other religious activities, like our families did at home. That said, those who wished to explore faith in greater depth were given the space to do so.

On my first Sunday afternoon at SAJOMACO, which was largely spent hanging around Wolex's room, I noticed some students who were walking to the chapel.

'Why are those guys heading to the chapel?' I asked.

'Bible study', he replied. 'There's a group that runs in the afternoon, between lunch and supper'.

'Thank goodness we're free from having to do yet more Bible study. Just imagine if Dad and Mum were here. They would force us to go'.

'I've got news for you'.

'What news?'

'We're going to the Bible study. Yes, you and me'.

'I'm not going. I don't have to go. You can't force me. We had service this morning. I did my devotion this morning already. That's enough for one day. No one's going to be the boss of me. You can go if you want'.

'The sessions give you more perspective', he explained. 'It's called Bible *study* for a reason. And there are older, more mature students there. I've found that it has helped me, especially on some big life questions. And I should also add, the fellowship is a good thing. We all need friends. I reacted exactly like you in my first week'.

'So how come you eventually started going?'

'I didn't really have an option. Senior Kay just told me to follow him. He didn't ask if I wanted to go. He's my room head. He's not someone you get into a debate with'.

At that moment, Senior Kay walked in.

'Are you both ready?'

'Yes, Senior Kay', Wolex replied, jumping off the bunk.

'Bunmi, looks like you're more sensible than Wolex. You should have seen his face this time last year when I told him to follow me to Bible study'.

I did my best to force a fake smile.

Wolex was right. The Bible study group did have a positive impact on my life. But it also revealed the chasm between the faiths, and the potential for division.

Mozzy was one of the boys in our class study group. He was quite bright and a positive influence in the group. Yet, by our third year, we rarely interacted with him, because according to his interpretation of his faith, he was required to distance himself from us because we had fundamentally disparate theological views. This was very different from the culture I had grown up with, where people of different faiths interacted, despite their differences. It was a poignant lesson to me that differences of opinion, especially when they affect our worldviews or morality, could shatter the overly naive, optimistic view we had as starry eyed first-year students when we began our SAJOMACO journey.

***

Unlike visiting days, half-term break was better because we could leave the school grounds for home on a Thursday afternoon, to return on Sunday. Even some students whose homes were as far away as Lagos made the journey back home. It was a much-needed break from SAJOMACO grounds – a time to recuperate and recharge.

The school turned into a ghost campus during half-term but a few students usually stayed back when home was too far away. For these students, although nothing could replace an escape back to their homes, having a break on campus was still something to relish. During those few days, there were no prep classes and the staff left the students to their own devices. There was also an abundance of food.

For those students who made the journey home, while many were picked up by their parents or relatives, a significant number used public transport. In Nigeria speak, I was unashamedly part of the sheltered or 'buttered' group of students, referring to sandwiches containing at least a spread of butter or margarine, as opposed to poorer families who couldn't afford sandwiches. During my primary school years at OAU, our parents either drove us or we walked on OAU campus. For a brief period, some bus shuttles did run on the university campus. These were much safer than the commercial buses that plied the routes in Ile-Ife town, outside the university campus. We never once rode those buses.

As we moved through the years at SAJOMACO, we got bolder, and tried to water down our buttered status. One major opportunity came in the first term of my third year, towards the end of 1992. Christmas was only a few weeks away. We couldn't wait to go home.

'I heard that the teachers are going on strike soon', said Bykes.

Tee looked at him.

'Hmm, where did you hear that? I'm sure it's a rumour'.

'I heard it from Tolu'.

'You can't believe a word that comes out of that boy's mouth', I said.

'But haven't you noticed that the teachers are not really showing up for classes anymore? It's as if they've given up for the term, or they know something we don't know'.

Although we were hesitant to believe the rumour, we all secretly wished this one were true. A strike happening this close to the end of term meant we were unlikely to resume till the New Year, even if the strike were called off within a few days.

The rumour turned out to be true. We were informed at assembly the next day that the term was to end abruptly that day, and that all students had to leave the campus. Being inside SAJOMACO walls shielded us from the reality on the outside, unless one was amongst the lucky few with telephones at home. Even with that, we still needed permission to use the school telephone.

Within thirty minutes of the assembly being dismissed, cars began to arrive. The strike was already public. It just took longer for the news to reach us. Many of the students, including the OAU group, were operating in a vacuum because we could not communicate with our parents. We had no idea whether they were aware of the news and were on their way, or not. And, so, we waited. After a few hours, everyone left began making alternative plans. Those who had relatives in nearby towns chose to make their way to them. That wasn't an option for Wolex and me, because we didn't know of any relatives in Ondo State. Through the dust clouds kicked up by the arriving cars, several times a faint outline of a car resembling ours would emerge, causing us to react in excitement and relief, only to realise, once it got closer, that it was a false positive.

Wolex grew impatient.

'We need to leave too'.

'You can't be serious'. I snapped. 'You're joking, right?'

'No, I'm not. We don't know if every parent is aware of this strike. I don't want us to be left behind on campus. And with the school shut, there's no food'.

'But how are we going to get home? We've never even taken public transport in Ile-Ife'. I shook my head. 'It's too risky. I'm sure our parents would have made a plan. There's still time', I pleaded.

'Look around. How many students are left – maybe a hundred? We can't wait around. We need to head into town', he urged.

'Do we even know where to take the bus from?'

'We'll ask'.

'Do we have enough money?'

'Yes, I'm sure you have enough left over from visiting day'.

Luckily for us, the last visiting day had been just the previous week, so we did have enough cash for the journey.

This was not the first time Wolex and I differed on risk-taking. Three years earlier, our parents had driven both of us to an examination centre in Ondo town, about sixty kilometres from Ile-Ife. They left us with 10 naira as pocket money. After the exam, while we waited for them, Wolex decided to spend all the money on snacks. I argued with him that the money likely included some spare cash for emergencies. He responded that if that was the case, our parents would have been explicit. Reluctantly, and since he was older, I went along with his executive decision only to be subjected to the telling-off of our lives when our parents later found out what we had done.

'It's probably going to take us five hours to get to Ile-Ife, so if we're going to make the journey, we need to leave now', Wolex said. 'We don't want to be getting to Ile-Ife at dusk'.

My resistance dissipated. It was a valid point, and I didn't want to consider travelling in the dark. There were no streetlights between the towns. Also, the student population was thinning before our eyes. By 1:30 p.m., only a handful of students remained, including one of our OAU friends, Yega. The others had found their way out somehow. We had to leave.

Wolex and I were generally clueless about the journey ahead, and decided to follow some students whom we knew were heading to Akure, the capital of Ondo State. There was no direct bus to Ile-Ife. They all stopped in Akure.

We walked with our luggage for about thirty minutes to a filling station which doubled as a bus terminal, or garage, in Nigeria speak. The bus wouldn't leave until all the seats were occupied, which meant we had to sit and wait. When we got to Akure, we asked where we could take a bus to Ile-Ife. Unbeknown to us, the Ife garage was on the other side of town. That meant taking another bus, and spending more unbudgeted cash. Despite being novices, we ended up in in Ile-Ife five hours later, relieved.

Earlier that year, my family had moved out of OAU campus grounds to a new house that our parents had built in Ile-Ife town. Now, two malnourished boys, wheeling their suitcases on untarred roads was a sight to behold. We did not fit in with the rough and tumble set-up and market stalls bustling with vendors around us. A friend of our parents spotted us and ended our misery by giving us a lift. Our parents were beyond shocked when they saw us.

'Thank you *o*! Where did you find them?' Mum asked the kind lady who had given us the lift.

'At the junction'.

'I'm confused. Children, where have you come from? How did you get here from school?'

I whispered to Wolex that this was his moment to shine, that I'd leave all the explaining to him. He ignored me.

'We decided to take public transport when the school announced it was shutting down because of the strike', he began.

'But didn't you realise it was dangerous? There's a reason we drive you to school and come and pick you up from there', she lectured.

'When we didn't see you or Dad and the school literally emptied within a few hours—'

'Emptied. Literally. Really?'

'He's right, Mum', I said. 'We risked either staying behind and being stuck there without food and not knowing whether anyone was going to come and get us, or leaving'.

'How about your friends?'

'Everyone else left', Wolex said, 'although we left Yega there'.

'See? We had already made arrangements. Yega's dad was supposed to bring you. I just hope he's not worried sick about you leaving without him'.

We didn't have a response. I gave Wolex a side glance.

A year later, Bykes and I decided to embark on a similar journey to Akure to spend our half-term with his uncle who was the Principal of St Matthias College. Our justification was that his younger brother, Topsy, who by then had joined us at SAJOMACO, had been ill for a while and needed medical attention. During half-term, our health clinic was non-existent. So, we were even more emboldened.

A rushed-through but well-policed rule preventing students from leaving the campus had been in force for a few months. Many unruly students flouted this rule, even during normal term time, risking suspension or even expulsion. We chose not to associate with this group. However, during half-term, our eagerness to exit the campus led us to decide that the rule should not apply for that brief period. So, Bykes and I scaled the fence and arrived at St Matthias just over an hour later.

After depicting something close to a major crisis about Topsy's health, Bykes's uncle dispatched a Peugeot Station Wagon to SAJOMACO with Bykes' aunty and us to rescue Topsy. Three hours after we'd come up with the plan, Bykes, Topsy, and I were relaxing at St Matthias, enjoying half-term, away from SAJOMACO. We were becoming more street smart.

Nasa, me, Wolex and Yemsta (1986)

Grandma, Wolex, Yemsta, Nasa, me and Aunty Victoria (1989)

II

Part Two | Rules of Engagement

*'Think not to match yourself against the gods, for
men that walk the earth cannot hold their own with
the immortals.'*
— Homer

Chapter 7

The official line the school authorities propagated, especially to parents, was that all students had equal rights on campus. As far as our experience went, this was pure propaganda. All students may have been equal, but some were more equal than others.

Student life functioned within a relatively well-defined hierarchy. The sixth-year students – the most senior – occupied the top of the food chain. The nobodies were the shortest, first-year students. A first-year student's world was dominated by second- or third-year students. But if a fourth-year student suddenly showed up, they assumed the alpha male position, although other seniors were still relevant to some degree.

This unwritten rule – that respect for the senior students is paramount – was a code of conduct which governed the lives of students and kept proceedings and student life in order. To be ignorant of or indifferent to it was to willingly invite trouble on oneself.

Yoruba culture demands that children not address their elders by their first names. Some families extended this to siblings, but many OAU parents, who had imbibed western culture, did not. They did not encourage the sibling rule of a

'Brother' or 'Sister' prefix before an older sibling's first name.

Upon starting at SAJOMACO, I carried on as I would at home, addressing Wolex by name, only to have some of his friends and a few of the older seniors call me out. Even if Wolex had insisted I carry on with the status quo, we were no match for the student body's code. The culture was just too powerful. Wolex became Brother Wolex, as opposed to Senior Wolex, to distinguish his relationship to me from that of other seniors. I dropped this prefix like a wet soap bar the moment we left the grounds of SAJOMACO for holidays.

I once had a major falling out with Wolex in front of several students in my room. He accused me of being rude. He responded by giving me the dirtiest slap I have ever received from anyone. I did not see it coming. My entire being was screaming an eye for an eye, but I somehow restrained myself from lunging at him, despite the humiliation. I knew very well that if I tried to respond, the other seniors would discipline me severely for breaking the respect code. I muttered under my breath that I would get him back during the holidays. But when the time came, the desire to strike back had gone.

My first sobering experience interacting with seniors happened on a prep night in my first year. The school authorities did not restrict us to specific classrooms for prep, so I decided to head to Wolex's classroom.

We were relieved when the gong of the bell could be heard, ending prep at the scheduled 9:00 p.m. As we trooped out of the class, someone interrupted us, calling out Wolex's name. I turned around and recognised a scruffy-looking senior, Senior Jega. He stayed in the same extension dormitory of Vining House as my friend Tee. He was wearing a dishevelled brown house-wear shirt on top of his light-blue class-wear shorts.

'Yes, you', he barked, pointing at Wolex. 'Where is the bucket of water I asked for?'

'I've had no time to go to the reservoir', Wolex replied.

'What kind of attitude is that? You're going to pay for this, if I don't get my water'.

'I had to fetch three buckets for other seniors, so I didn't have time'.

'Are you saying I am not important enough to you?'

Wolex's face depicted a thousand words. I was itching to say something, but I had observed enough madness on campus already to realise that any word I uttered could get me into trouble, and make matters worse.

Wolex kept quiet and stared at his feet, hoping this episode would end quickly.

'Look at me!'

Wolex turned to look in his direction but didn't make eye contact. Senior Jega lunged at him, and shoved him in the chest with both hands.

'I said look at me!'

Wolex may have been powerless against Senior Jega, but whatever pride he had left was worth protecting. He refused to make eye contact.

'That's it! You'll be fetching one bucket per day for the rest of the week'.

By now, a crowd had gathered. Senior Jega was in the third year, just a year ahead of Wolex. He pulled Wolex by the collar of his shirt and started to drag him away, no doubt to put him through some humiliating punishment.

Watching this drama was excruciating for me. Despite the brotherly competition between us, there was only so much I could take of what this bully was doing to my big brother.

My head told me I had to keep my mouth shut, but my heart wasn't having any of it.

'He told you already he didn't have the time to do it. You can see his left hand too, can't you?' I cried.

Wolex's left arm is slightly deformed, and has been since birth. Before SAJOMACO, it often worked as a perfect get-out-of-jail card. Not now, not with our seniors.

Senior Jega ignored me. My tiny voice must have sounded like a mouse's squeak in the background. With tears trickling down my face, I did my best to keep up. A fifth-year student happened to be walking towards us. Once he got close enough, he could make out our faces. I recognised him as Senior Apache.

Senior Jega abruptly let go of Wolex's shirt.

'Jega, is that you?'

'Yes'.

'Where's my bucket of water? Or you think I've forgotten? Or that I wouldn't find you on this campus?'

'Sorry. I didn't have time to get it because I had to run an errand for Senior Yode. He told me you'd understand'.

I couldn't believe my ears.

'You should have sent a message to me to explain'.

'Sorry, again'.

'Anyway, what has this boy done to you?'

Silence.

Wolex grabbed his chance.

'He told me to fetch water. I explained I didn't have time, because I had to do the same thing for other seniors, but he still wants to punish me'.

'Is this true?'

'He's just making excuses. The boy is lying *jare*'.

68

'So, you couldn't be reasonable with him, yet you expect me to be nice to you. Isn't it funny? This situation reminds me of one of the parables in the New Testament – or is it the Old Testament? Anyway, it doesn't matter. If I'm not mistaken, the character in that parable who was like you, Jega, ended up in jail, or something like that. Luckily for you, everybody knows Apache is a good guy. I won't break your legs or anything like that. For that, you should be grateful. How about this? From now on, you will fetch me a bucket of water every day for the rest of the term. If I hear that you cause this little boy any more grief, I'll double your punishment. What is that saying again? "What goes around…"'

His voice trailed off as he disappeared into the darkness. An infuriated Senior Jega stormed off also.

I could only imagine what Wolex's evening would have been like without Senior Apache's intervention. Although we were both relieved that Wolex was free, the fear that Senior Jega might try to get his own back later, somehow, was difficult to suppress.

Some students rebelled in such situations, hoping to challenge the normal order, but any progress they made was usually temporary. For example, a second-year student might disrespect a third-year student because the former enjoyed protection from a fourth- or fifth-year student. But that protection had an expiry date. Once the fourth- or fifth-year student graduates, the third-year student would inevitably seek retribution. Forgiveness was not built into the code.

While the code was very beneficial for seniors, a few took its enforcement to the extreme, tapping into the darkest parts of their soul, behaving like dictators. The most common tasks for juniors involved fetching water and washing plates and clothes. Beyond the chores assigned to juniors, many seniors also designated specific juniors to run errands for them. This was akin to a master–slave type relationship. Some seniors forced second- or third-year students to perform tasks usually carried out by first-year students. During my fourth year, Baji, one of the most feared sixth-year students, walked into my room. He pointed at me.

'You, what's your name?'

'Bunmi Asaolu'.

'Take this plate, wash it, and submit it to the dining hall. You will be doing this until further notice'.

That was the start of a high-risk job that yielded decidedly more potential problems for me than benefits. The benefits were rare, but they did occur from time to time when Baji chose to give me his meal. To his credit, he fulfilled his side of his bargain – not making my life hell – while I fulfilled mine. However, I would rather have been free and content with the one plate of food I was rightly entitled to than be his slave. But I had no choice.

My first experience of the naivety of juniors regarding breaking the respect code was during lunch at the dining hall a few weeks after arriving at SAJOMACO. The Principal joined us for lunch. Once he decided that he had given enough time for students to arrive and take their seats, he instructed the prefects to lock all the doors. I felt sorry for those who were locked out, because some students did have genuine reasons for their late arrival. Sadly, SAJOMACO proceedings were usually harsh. The teachers and prefects dismissed excuses, believing they were phoney. The Principal stood up and prayed, 'Bless this food, O Lord, for Christ's sake!'

The students chorused, 'Amen!'

That was followed by the clanging and clashing of plate covers being removed and students tucking into their meal. Relative calm followed. The hall was more orderly and quieter than normal because of the Principal factor.

After most students had eaten their lunch, the Principal stood up. We assumed he was going to say the closing prayer, ask the prefects to open the doors, and allow the latecomers to come in. The delayed lunch wouldn't kill them, and at least they would have learned a lesson.

'Students, I hope you enjoyed your meal?'

'Yes, sir'.

'Sometimes I hear one or two complaints about the food we give you. I think you'll agree with me that this was an excellent meal'.

Of course, it wasn't like he was asking for genuine feedback.

'I have noticed that some students, particularly the older ones, think they have two heads. To them, coming to the dining hall to eat is beneath them. So, they send a junior to ferry their plates to and from the dining hall. Well, today I have news for them'.

Murmuring could be heard. What was the Principal up to? He must have something up his sleeve – some punishment of some sort.

'I am not going to let them open those doors', he said, pointing to the prefects.

By now, many students who had been shut out of the hall were peeking through the windows, their faces pressed against the burglary proof. Some were mouthing instructions to other students, friends, to prevent their plates of food, sitting there yet untouched, from being seized.

'Thank you, Lord, for the food we have just eaten'.

'Amen'.

The Principal gave the order that any untouched plates of food were to be consumed on the premises. The students coined a word for the takeover of another student's plate of food: *cantab*. Everyone had equal access to any unclaimed plate. The juniors responded quickest. To them, there was no reason to second-guess what their bellies were telling them to do, given that the order came from the person with the most authority on campus. They wasted no time gobbling up food belonging to a latecomer, as those latecomers looked on.

Some of the seniors locked outside the hall could see which juniors consumed their food, while others who had stayed behind in the dormitories found out by word of mouth. The punishment was swift. In addition to the beatings the juniors received, some of them had to pay back the seniors in the form of multiple lunches in the days ahead. The seniors taught the juniors a crucial lesson: a *cantab* order, regardless of who gave it, should not be applied to a senior's plate of food.

For most of my time at SAJOMACO, students submitted their own plates to the dining hall. They were responsible for cleaning and resubmitting them. If a senior's plate went missing for any reason, the wrath of the senior fell squarely on the junior.

The Principal's *cantab* order didn't change the behaviour of the seniors. By my third year, their obsession with doing a no-show at the dining hall became so pervasive that teachers began to show up unannounced for lunch to confront the habit head-on. Once the doors were locked, staff would position themselves outside the doors of the hall and inspect the students as they exited.

Inspecting a flood of students as they filed out of the dining hall was not straightforward. To do so properly would have been time consuming. Consequently, the approach taken was not watertight, which encouraged the juniors to take risks. Some of them exited the hall through the rear doors; these were not always guarded properly because they led out into an area where the kitchen, a storeroom, and one of the bathrooms were situated. When using this back route, students had to take a long-winded route around the tennis court on one side or the lavatory, the Arts building, and then one of two large water reservoirs to avoid being spotted. Not all succeeded. Some of the cannier teachers could spot a gnat from a mile away and would swiftly dispatch one of the prefects to hunt down the escaping student.

Another elusive approach the students devised involved holding their plates in a sloppy, slanting manner, hoping to fool the teachers into thinking their plates were empty. Some students strapped plates of food to their bodies just above their buttocks and covered them with their free-flowing shirts. Perhaps the most daring plan involved students pretending they were returning to the dormitory from the bathroom. Walking with a bucket in hand and a towel wrapped around the hip was a good enough camouflage. The plate of food was placed inside the bucket and a soap box placed on top of it to conceal it.

Despite their best plans, many students failed to get past the teachers. Even though the risks were high, a food runner for a senior would go to any length to smuggle food out of the dining hall. There was no special reward for this bravery. It was simply expected. If caught, the minimum punishment was the emptying of the plate of food onto the dirt, right in front of everyone.

Chapter 8

Some seniors believed it was their God-given duty to make juniors grow up. Errands were a favoured tool they employed. A typical scenario played out like this:

Senior Jay might say, 'Ope, go to Okusanya House Room 4. Ask for Bado. Tell him that I asked you to collect my *arodan* from him'.

'Yes, Senior Jay', Ope would reply. 'I'll go right away'. And Ope would head off to Bado.

This request by Senior Jay could sometimes be intended as a punishment for Ope. At other times, it was just because Senior Jay felt like it. The immediate challenge Ope faced was not knowing whether Bado was his senior or junior, so, before going to Okusanya House, he would do his homework and find out that Bado was in the same year as Senior Jay. Potential disaster averted! Calling Bado by just his name would most definitely have compounded the misery of his day.

'Good afternoon, Senior Bado', Ope would say. 'Senior Jay sent me to collect his *arodan* from you'.

'Oh, that stuff. Let me see. Em… I think I gave it to Kunta Kinte'.

Unfortunately, Kunta Kinte would be on the other side of the school grounds, playing football, but Senior Bado somehow knew of his whereabouts. Convenient.

An hour later and Ope would find that this *arodan* was just one more errand away.

There were a number of ways this 'errand-athon' ended: one of the seniors either read between the lines, or directly, that Ope had been on the case of the *arodan* for some time and felt it was time to have mercy on his soul, or Ope started to smell a rat, made enquiries by himself, and discovered this was just a run-around, and that Senior Bado, and the rest of the seniors who played along, simply set him up for the fun of it. Or he happened to find out accidentally through a friend that there is no such thing as an *arodan*.

For juniors like Ope, it was a race against time to catch up with the unwritten rules that governed student life. Naivety could be costly – physically, emotionally, and financially. Juniors tended to get into the most amount of trouble in their first weeks at SAJOMACO, when their lockers would be overflowing, having arrived on campus with all the gadgets the school had requested they show up with. In contrast, the lockers owned by the seniors were bare. Only essential items made it into their lockers – toiletries and food with a long shelf-life. Seniors deemed the so-called necessities the school demanded of the students a luxury. In my early years at SAJOMACO, teachers carried out inspections to check that students had the items on the required list, but by the time I graduated the inspections were a thing of the past.

Once the sun set and darkness descended on the school grounds, the natural instinct of a first-year student was to grab a flashlight as he left the dormitory. Seniors usually didn't have flashlights. They were more likely to be found with kerosene lanterns – if they had any form of lighting at all. Outdoor lighting was generally poor, even during the periods when the school managed to draw on the epileptic power supply from the grid.

For most juniors, their first night at SAJOMACO was their first ever using a flashlight outdoors, one they actually owned. The realisation was a real confidence booster. Marching down the walkways from the dormitories, the flashlights helped the students explore and sate their curiosity. It was almost inevitable that what was supposed to have brought some spark to a junior's night-time experience would make life complicated once he crossed paths with a senior, especially if the rays of light were directed straight at the latter's face.

'You, over there with the flashlight. Come here! Give me that flashlight right now!'

There was virtually no escape. Although technically not impossible, it was very difficult for a junior to outrun a senior. Fear would paralyse the junior before the thought of running even crossed his mind. The more sensible juniors would follow the senior around for as long as it took, begging all the way, before risking collecting a beating. There was no guarantee that this strategy would work. The most ignorant juniors would have been in a state of shock, completely paralysed to even begin to process what had just happened. For many juniors, this marked the last time they would ever see their flashlights.

If a junior successfully navigated the flashlight ordeal, other pitfalls lay ahead. Seniors generally had very little of anything useful that could lead to the betterment of their lives in school. Their thinking went along the lines of: *Why flood the school with similar gadgets, from flashlights to kerosene lanterns to mathematical sets, when there were hundreds of gullible juniors who would show up with these same items anyway? One could always 'borrow' from them.*

Lending anything to a senior came with huge risks, because there was no collateral behind this loan. The rights of the senior were far superior. In fact, to be blunt, the junior's rights were limited to the understanding that he owned the item in question. But if there was any disagreement regarding this act of goodwill from the junior, the word of the senior would prevail in any student gathering that resembled a court. The harsh truth was: the senior is always right. He might show mercy and return the item undamaged, and within a reasonable time, but there were no guarantees. There were countless cases of lanterns, soap bars, cutlery, buckets, money, and so on and so forth being 'gifted' away, despite weeks, even months, of the owner requesting the items back.

Some seniors took the respect culture to such an extreme that it became difficult to see it any other way than as pure wickedness. The actions of these seniors baffled us, because it was difficult to understand how they reasoned their actions were sane. The argument that it was to toughen up or mature us was a lame one.

A very common story, repeated over the years, involved seniors asking juniors to head over to the school tuck shop, or canteen as it was called, to purchase some items. The cash given to the juniors barely covered the price of the items.

'Oh, I forgot to add, bring half the amount I gave you back, as change', the senior might add, as a parting shot.

Lennon House was known for housing the worst-behaved students on campus. It was difficult to say whether it was a case of bad habits being passed down from one year to the next, or there was something nasty about Lennon House itself that led to its reputation. It consistently held the title for worst offences and maltreatment of juniors. It was also in Lennon House that one of the rooms was converted into a hot food canteen outlet, of sorts. The seniors in this room would scale the school fence – an extremely serious offence – to buy food from Mama Sumbo's canteen, situated opposite the school's side gate, and sell it to students. The complementary protein of choice was fried fish, which sold for a tidy premium.

Seniors patronised this illegal Lennon House canteen. When it ran out of food, some seniors would demand that the juniors they had sent to buy food on their behalf not return empty-handed. Apart from preventing these juniors from studying, demand for these errands usually peaked at night, during prep, and some juniors were forced to illegally scale the school fence to get the job done. The callousness these seniors showed seemed to have no limits.

There were times, however, when the subculture was challenged, but it inevitably came with consequences. During my fourth year, two brothers who had failed their final-year exams in another school enrolled to retake the exams at SAJOMACO. It appeared to us that this was not the first retake for them. Given that they were older than the sixth-year students, they generally kept out of everybody's business and operated in their own bubble. However, after a couple of months, they started to establish a new order which was at odds with the subculture on campus. They disrespected some sixth-year students and effectively put themselves over and above the most senior students on campus.

Things came to a head when word spread that the brothers had punished a sixth-year student. Following that, we learned that they had subjected some of the younger sixth-year students to the types of menial tasks usually reserved for juniors.

The rest of the sixth-year students had been watching and noting these developments, but looked the other way, convincing themselves that their affected classmates had brought whatever they were experiencing on their own heads. Their attitude changed when they heard how the two brothers had punished their classmate.

A few of the most feared sixth-year students held an impromptu crisis meeting after it was discovered that the two brothers had left the school for Owo town earlier that day. Leaving the school grounds was a privilege that was only extended to the sixth-year students when their final exams were close. However, for some unknown reason, these two brothers switched between being boarders and day students, whenever they felt like it.

A plan was hatched to confront them on their return the next day. Some students were so afraid of the two brothers that they kept cutlasses under their mattresses as they slept that night. At around 5:00 p.m., the brothers were spotted walking up the 200-metre approach into the boys' dormitory area from the main gate. Tension filled the air. Experienced students could read the situation well merely by observing the random pattern of the movement of students supposedly going about their normal business.

The brothers were housed in Akinyele House. They turned right at the top of the school entrance approach, a vantage point from where there was a good view of the boys' dormitory and parts of Owo town. They covered another fifty metres and were soon next to the main water reservoir to their right.

Suddenly, about a hundred and fifty metres away in the

distance, students could be seen charging down from Vining House towards the brothers. At the same time, the sound of students rushing down the wooden staircase of Akinyele House could be heard. The two brothers sensed all was not well, as the noise grew louder. When one of the angry seniors reached the brothers, he confronted them and a heated argument broke out. Spectators gathered around the balcony of Akinyele House to witness this live blockbuster of a show.

One of the brothers landed a well-executed slap on the face of the senior, while the other brother reached out and grabbed his throat. Another senior, nicknamed Jaja, a reference to a local Benin Kingdom warrior, who had rushed down the stairs of Akinyele House, appeared, armed with the broken leg of a chair.

'Drop your hand!' Jaja ordered.

'And if I don't?'

'Drop your hand. I won't say it again'.

'Do your worst'.

Jaja took aim, swung with all the adrenaline pumping through his body, and landed the chair-leg-turned-weapon on the brother's arm. Watching this episode was painful enough. It was hard to imagine what it must have felt like to be on the receiving end. Still, the brother did not let go of the senior's throat until a second hit landed. The arm was probably fractured, but the brothers did not hang around after the episode was over for anyone to find out.

By this time the Vining House students had arrived, landing blows on the brothers. They resisted, but were no match for the growing number of students who had descended on them. This was mob justice at its worst, with potentially deadly consequences.

The mob showed no mercy. Unfortunately for the brothers, they had alienated so many students that even the neutrals were either standing by, remaining neutral or agreeing with the unfolding attack. Some joined the fray, throwing stones, bricks, cudgels – anything deadly they could lay their hands on. As missiles rained down on the brothers, they were left with no choice but to run for their lives. One dashed to the staff building where, fortunately, a few teachers were present. The second brother made for the farm and eventually disappeared into the bush. It was safer getting lost in the bush and risk serious injury from booby traps set for rodents and game than to experience the full wrath of a very angry mob of students.

The brothers did sit their final exams at SAJOMACO, albeit with some level of staff protection. However, they did not spend another night on campus.

The other notable example of external groups challenging the subculture involved parents trying to meddle in the affairs of students. In theory, there was general agreement that bullying and mistreatment of students was inappropriate and should not be allowed. In practice, however, the reality was very different. When a parent of a bullied student was confronted with this truth, the natural response was for the parent to give the senior a stern rebuke. Threats would be made by the parent; the seniors who made the life of the junior a living hell were warned that they would be reported to the school authorities and punished. Sometimes, the rebuke of the senior was done in public. Though rare, a parent or two slapped the senior.

It was a hard pill to swallow for parents hearing of their child being bullied, for three reasons. First, the atrocities were sometimes extreme. Second, they couldn't prevent it from happening by being so far away from the school. Third, the oldest of these so-called seniors were mere teenagers – children.

The uncomfortable truth was that a bullied junior still had to navigate life on campus alone after any dressing-down of a senior was done – without the parents. Then what? If the parent had thrown a mega tantrum, the student subculture would ultimately prevail. If the parent had gone too far in rebuking the senior, some 'anonymous' students would mete out even worse bullying on the junior. And the senior would have a perfect alibi to show that he had nothing to do with this new pain being experienced by the junior. The spate of physical attacks on the junior would increase, his room chores would grow exponentially, and theft of his belongs would skyrocket.

If students were to advise the parents, unanimously, they would suggest diplomacy over a shock-and-awe or show-of-force approach. Even the most senior students on campus who could provide protection for the junior towed this line, because they knew that any cover they gave for the junior would expire once they themselves graduated.

Stoking the ego of a senior who was a bully generally worked. Some parents were able to convert a bully into a big brother character who then went out of his way to protect the same junior he had previously oppressed.

When diplomacy failed, the only options left were for the junior to bear the pain until the senior graduated or to move to another school. Often, the abused would himself become a worse abuser, maltreating his juniors and growing into an even worse tyrant. Thankfully, others chose nobler paths, demonstrating that it was possible to end the bullying cycle.

Chapter 9

The culture of respect is steeped in the Nigerian psyche. After parents, masters – teachers – were next in the hierarchy. Truancy and rebellion rarely surfaced in primary school, but they found fertile ground to grow in secondary school. Add in a small dose of peer pressure, hormones, and puberty, and you had a potent mix.

Although I have fond memories of some of our teachers, like Mrs Olagbegi and Reverend Dahunsi, it was decidedly a minority group. In boarding school, rumours, lies, and the actions of some teachers helped perpetuate the view that, as a group, teachers were not to be trusted. Beyond the classroom, our teachers appeared to be too busy with their own lives and families to really care about us.

To be fair, the pressure they were under as a result of Nigeria's worsening economic situation was a lot to deal with. However, even as far back as my first year, when Nigeria was not on its knees, we were still suspicious of our teachers. At the very least, the goings-on on campus did not help foster a bond between us. While we did not completely believe our parents' assertion that our teachers were the panacea to our issues, the reality of life on campus made it easy for us to castigate our teachers and blame them for the difficulties that life threw our way. By entrusting our lives to the teachers on campus, our parents took risks, even if they didn't admit it. Some students discovered the dark side to our teachers the painful way.

Ojugo was a good friend of Bykes, my classmate from OAU. Both lived in Okusanya House. Their friendship had grown over table football. Ojugo usually won the prize money, without contributing a single kobo to the pot. He preyed on our desperation, because he knew that the tournament was more exciting when many students participated. The entry fee was two naira. For some reason, Ojugo never had any money on him, repeating that his 'two naira was in his room' every time. He'd suggest that we put him down as owing, and that he'd make good the winner by paying that person directly. Except, because he kept on winning, he never had to prove that the two naira was not imaginary.

Riding on a win from one of these tournaments, Ojugo strode gallantly towards the dining hall. By this time, our typical dining hall experience had become chaotic, with plates of food consistently being stolen or destroyed. The teachers intervened out of necessity by changing the system from a sit-down meal to a pick-your-plate-and-go approach. Mr Lalupon was the master in charge that evening. He and the prefects ordered us to line up by year group. Each student would enter the hall, pick up their plate, and exit from the hall's rear. Once the process shifted to the next year group, any late student ran the risk of forfeiting his food.

On his way to the hall, Ojugo crossed paths with an infamous senior in the fifth year.

'Ojugo!'

'Yes, Senior Keregbe'.

'I need a favour. Are you my guy?'

'Hmm, OK'.

'What kind of answer is that? Don't you want to live to your old age? Hmm is not what I need currently. You and I must be on the same parallelogram. *Sho* get?'

Ojugo stared down at his slippers. They had seen better days; he had re-stitched them at least five times.

'I can't find anyone to do this job for me. The Lord has clearly brought you my way. I need you to get my plate from the hall and bring it to my room'.

'But…'

'But what? Do you want to live? Or die? Bring the plate to my room!'

With that, Senior Keregbe strode off, leaving poor Ojugo contemplating what awaited him. Could he possibly sneak into the dining hall a second time to pick up Senior Keregbe's plate without being noticed? Or maybe the other way round was safer: retrieve Senior Keregbe's plate before his own.

'Next class, your turn!'

There was no time to analyse the situation. Ojugo darted into line, shuffled his way along the tables once he got into the hall, picked up his plate, and made for the exit. Once he got out, he gave his plate to a friend.

'Hold it for me. I have no time to explain…' Ojugo turned and sprinted around the block and back to the entrance. He pulled out his shirt, which had been neatly tucked in earlier, and undid his buttons in a desperate attempt to disguise himself. Avoiding eye contact, he walked forward, briskly, only for a giant hand to grab his upper left arm and pull him aside at the last minute.

'You've picked up your plate already, haven't you?' Mr

Lalupon challenged, looking straight into his eyes.

'I… I have…, I haven't, sir. Honestly, I'm telling the truth'.

'So, why are you nervous then?'

'I'm… I'm not nervous, sir'. Ojugo's stuttering was too much of a giveaway.

'See this thief? I will make an example of you'.

'Sorry, sir', he gasped. 'It's a senior that made me line up again, sir. Please, I beg you…'

Mr Lalupon grabbed hold of Ojugo's collar, almost suffocating the poor soul, pressing hard on his Adam's apple.

'Please, sir, have mercy', he choked.

He would get a flogging, as a minimum, no question. But his pleading further infuriated Mr Lalupon.

Wham!

Like a boxer on the end of an unexpected knockout punch from an opponent, Ojugo's head snapped to one side. Mr Lalupon's hands were a good prop for a Biology lesson on evolution. One could have easily mistaken them for an orangutan's. But this was not the kind of specimen anyone should see connecting with a twelve-year-old's face.

'My eyes!' he shrieked. *'Ye!* My eyes!'

Wham!

Another slap.

'I'll slap that *ole*[3] gene out of your body', Mr Lalupon shouted, his voice spilling over with righteous indignation.

Five minutes later, he had beaten Ojugo into a sorry pulp, Ojugo's shirt torn and soaking wet from a mixture of tears and sweat.

Ojugo's vision was blurred, even after his eyes had dried.

---

[3] Thief.

His vision did not improve that night. It never did. The next day, a jittery Mr Lalupon, now made aware of this, did his best to project a model master image, showing great care. Ojugo's parents were of means and worked for the government. Mr Lalupon's excessive punishment of Ojugo meant his job was probably on the line, and he knew it. Indeed, Ojugo's vision was now so bad that he was forced to leave campus for home. Later, we learned that Mr Lalupon travelled to see Ojugo's parents to plead with them.

Ojugo returned to campus, a pair of glasses now on his nose. He wore them for the rest of his time at school.

Mr Lalupon's begging had achieved its goal. He never faced a disciplinary hearing. To our amazement, he ended up fulfilling a quasi-guardian role for Ojugo, with his parents' blessing. Culture can conceal a multitude of sins.

***

The SAJOMACO chapel doubled as the school assembly hall. The original stone-structure was a quaint, modest-sized building, but sturdy nonetheless. By the time I enrolled at the school, two extension sections had been annexed, one on each side. The one which the girls sat in had been completed, but by completed, I mean it had a roof and the floor had been sand-filled. There were no funds to put in a concrete floor or tiles, like the original building had. The other extension, designated for the boys, was still being constructed at the start of my first year. The frame of the building and a deep cavity in the floor, which needed to be sand-filled, were apparent for all to see.

A week had not yet passed since I arrived at SAJOMACO

that, one afternoon, the school bell rang out, just after lunch. Normally when the bell rang like this, we knew it was for our manual labour work. The latter was a permanent fixture on Wednesday afternoons and Saturday mornings, the so-called labour days. The school compound was vast, covering several tens of hectares. In order to maintain a tidy appearance, in a tropical environment, clearing the vegetation was a full-time job, particularly in the wet season. During the holidays, the vegetation was left to grow wild, because hundreds of gardeners would have been required to tame it. The school just did not have the money to do the required landscaping work. As such, we cut the bushes on our labour days ourselves, using cutlasses.

Teachers showed little mercy to any student whose cutlass was lost, stolen, or damaged. Such a student had to rely on other students to lend him or her their cutlass.

It did not matter how thick or overgrown the bush was, or whether there were stinging nettles. Given the number of students unleashed, we eventually cleared the vegetation. Blisters on the palm from cutlass usage were a standard rite of passage, and if one developed a bad rash due to an allergic reaction, no one batted an eyelid, including the school authorities.

Japhy, our master in charge of labour duties, whose surname translates as 'one who stood with the Lord', was the centre of attention at labour gatherings. It did not take long before we concluded that the meaning of his surname was at odds with how he related to us. He had a reputation as a disciplinarian. He barked out instructions in lexicon which we barely under-stood. The previous day, at the start of labour activities, we observed him in full flow.

'Year One!'

'Yes, sir', we chorused.

'You, what's your name again?' he asked, pointing at one of the prefects with his long cane.

'Banji, sir'. He emerged from the pack of prefects and shuffled quickly towards Japhy. It was necessary to hear the instructions the first time. There wasn't going to be a repeat.

'Banji, take this group to the section next to the Staff room, perambulate down to the Principal's house, then glide all the way down to the girls' dining hall, capture the adjacent patch between the science blocks before bulldozing decisively to the back of the SS1 block. Off you go!'

Unlike the prefects, who were veterans, we were generally clueless about how small or extensive the area Japhy had described was, because we didn't know the grounds well. Prefects had enough experience to piece together the instructions, no matter how jumbled up Japhy's instructions were.

Given that there had been a labour session the previous day, it was strange that we were asked to assemble so soon after. But this time around, we were asked to bring a bucket, not a cutlass. School life was still pure adventure for us, so curiosity was enough to get us out of our dormitories. We assembled in front of Akinyele House, where the girls also joined us. We lined up according to our classes. A few teachers had turned up to supervise the task we were going to undertake, but Japhy was leading the charge.

'Today, the first-year students have some important work to do', he began. 'All of you must head to an excavation site behind Lennon House, in the boys' dormitory'.

A large mound of deep-red clay soil almost as tall as a first-year student had been dug up around the perimeter of what was to become a new pit latrine building.

'Your task is to carry as much of the clay at the back of Lennon House in your buckets all the way to the chapel. Your target is fifteen buckets each. You will have a team of supervisors closely watching you. Everybody must participate. If we catch you trying to sneak away or find that your bucket is only partially full, we will mark you down. Anyone who doesn't complete fifteen trips will lose their dinner'.

He paused to let the information sink in.

'Am I clear?'

'Yes, sir'.

We were shell-shocked. The school had turned us into labourers, to be used to sand-fill the second extension of the chapel!

With so many supervisors monitoring us, there was no time for chitchat or reflection on how much this back-breaking work was going to take out of us.

We later learned that the first extension of the chapel, the girls' section, had been filled by the older students before we arrived at SAJOMACO. There was no parent to appeal to in order to escape from this slave labour.

'Why didn't Wolex mention this to me?' I muttered, on my first leg to the chapel, feeling my neck being crushed by the weight of the earth on my head. Even more annoying was the fact that class captains, like Sage in my class, who were generally derided for being teachers' pets, were also drafted to join the supervisors' club. They stood at the chapel doors, looking smug in their neat clothes, while the rest of us toiled, our house wear coated with red dirt. Some had the cheek to mark some of our trips to the chapel as a half-trip, because they judged the buckets were not quite full to the brim. These guys were snakes – backstabbers, as far as we were concerned.

The chapel work became a permanent fixture of our afternoons over the weeks that followed, until we cleared the clay mound and filled the chapel extension. This was one of the first experiences that led us to conclude that our school was like a prison camp.

Our teachers would point to the fact that the school did not have the funds to hire workmen to do what they made us do. As far as we were concerned, this was not what we had signed up for.

Some teachers appeared to cherish their position of influence, seeming to get a thrill from the pain students experienced. Some of their actions probably spurned the legends and rumours that seniors propagated, like those about Mr Holly.

He was a relatively young master who had gained notoriety by sneaking up on students breaking school rules and giving them a serious beating. He moved with stealth, pouncing on unsuspecting victims with lightning speed. To help his camouflage, he had sown for himself a set of our house wear. He was known for stalking students who preferred to hang around the dormitories instead of heading to prep, with the intention of flushing them out. He also hovered around the classrooms during prep, seeking out students who had dozed off, to punish them.

Teachers were not duty-bound to herd students out of their dormitories for prep. In Mr Holly's case, it was a unilateral decision he took to conduct his espionage operations, although other teachers sometimes joined in. When they did, it felt like the dormitories were under attack. During the day, teachers might smile or joke with students. By dusk, they transformed into SAJOMACO's own crackdown agents.

The raids by the likes of Mr Holly formed the basis of some incredible stories which were passed down from one student generation to another. The gullible junior in me believed that some of these stories did, in fact, happen as told. It was said that on a particular evening, shortly before prep started, some students had been lying in wait for a certain teacher. Lighting was terrible in our dormitories. On the night in question, the lights in one of the extension dormitories had been deliberately switched off. The master approached quietly, and made his way into the building via the front entrance. Unknown to him, the students had set a trap in the form of a tripwire and some buckets of water overhead. The teacher tripped, fell facedown, and was completely drenched.

This story, and others like it, lacked one obvious conclusion: if these events really did happen, then the punishment that would have been meted out to the entire group of students in that dormitory – guilty or innocent – would have been on such a scale that generations of students would have heard about them and repeated the telling.

Stories about the origins of the nicknames given to teachers also did the rounds. While Fala was a pretty straightforward nickname, coined from a surname, the students decided to be adventurous with other names. Japhy, for Japheth, would have sufficed. Instead, sometimes, the students called him Japhytoto because it rolled off the tongue better and had more of a zing to it. If Peperempe had been given a dictionary definition, something along the lines of 'loud-mouth' or 'biggest mouth on the face of the earth' would have been recorded. It was the most appropriate nickname for the teacher, since he sounded like a megaphone all the time.

Most teachers eventually found out what their nicknames were. If this revelation was sprung on them by a student, a punishment usually followed swiftly, and, thereafter, a game of cat and mouse ensued as students covertly used the nickname and the teacher tried to enforce a zero-tolerance policy.

Mr Iji was our Agriculture teacher. He was a short man, almost bald, with protruding black-framed glasses plucked straight from the 1950s. On one occasion, I was told that upon meeting a group of students for the first time in class, he asked them to introduce themselves.

'Good afternoon, sir. My name is Tee Adeyinka'.

'Afternoon, sir, Adebola Potoki', the next student said.

'Tajudeen Ahmed, sir'.

'Uche Nwachukwu, sir'.

'Ernest Potoki'.

By the time all forty students had introduced themselves, for the first time in his teaching career, it dawned on him that unlike last names such as Taiwo, Ojo, and Nwosu, which were quite common, Pokoti was in a league of its own. It had become the de facto Smith or Jones equivalent. In this alleged instance, recalling some incidents he had witnessed over the previous days, Mr Iji reflected out loud. His comments were logged into the subconscious long-term memory of those students, to be replayed year in year out like a classic poem.

On my machine, Potoki.
  On the farm, Potoki.
  In the classroom, Potoki.
  At the gate, Potoki.
  On the field, Potoki.
  Who is this Potoki gan?

Like many stories symbolising the notoriety on campus, this Potoki account is likely closer to folklore than an actual event. However, when Mr Iji did ride his motorcycle around the campus, random shouts of 'Potoki' would ring out from some indistinct, shadowy corner of the boys' dormitory in his wake. I envisioned him cursing under his breath, wishing he could wring the necks of the culprits. The nickname stuck, like glue.

Chapter 10

One evening, during the first term of my fourth year, a group of students congregated in Room 7 of Akinyele House, my room. There was no rhyme or reason behind the genesis of this huddle. Because no one made the decision to leave for prep, the chatter and mingling continued well past the start of prep. Ours was not the only room ignoring prep.

Without warning, the mood changed. We suddenly heard voices of teachers descending on the dormitory. A raid was on, and the teachers were determined to make scapegoats of whomever they caught. We heard screams and the thundering sound of students running for their dear lives, as they were chased out of their rooms and flogged.

There was no time to assess the situation or dwell at length as to what we should do. My room head made an executive decision to switch the light off and ordered everyone to stay put and remain completely quiet. In less than a minute, Akinyele House was reduced to a ghost dormitory.

Either my room head was a genius or the most stupid senior on campus – we were about to find out. There were close to twenty of us crowded into a room designed to house four people on two bunk beds.

The play-dead plan began well. Whoever was outside hunting for students did not target our room. The ensuing quiet indicated that the plan might have worked. But it was still too risky to break cover, and even if we wanted to, we could easily misjudge it.

'Thank goodness! We got away with it', whispered someone.

'Shut up!' snapped a senior, hoarsely. 'They might still be around somewhere!'

'Nothing's going to happen. Can you hear anything?'

'If we get caught...'

The sound of footsteps in the hallway directly above us abruptly halted the whispers. Everyone froze.

We heard the door of the room above us open.

'I'm sorry, sir, I'm sorry', pleaded a student, clearly scared.

Whoosh!

We heard the lashing of the cane connecting with the unfortunate souls upstairs. It sent a cold chill down our spines.

Loud shrieks of pain were followed by footsteps as the students bolted and flew down the staircase. Students needed just a second to clear the flight of stairs. A firm grip with both arms on the bannister transitioned into a glide downward, as they leapfrogged down in one clean jump.

As the students in the above room made their escape, we stood in silence, waiting for the expected sound of the teacher leaving the room. Instead, he walked back and forth, the wooden planks above us creaking under his weight as he slowly made his way around the room. The longer he lingered there, the more apprehensive we got, as the ramifications of such a thorough search dawned on each of us.

'What if he decides to do a sweep of every room in the dormitory?' someone hissed.

We were able to track his movement because the planks of our ceiling had some narrow gaps, the result of years of wear and tear and lack of maintenance, making the rays from his flashlight visible. Normally, these gaps were just an inconvenience for the ground floor inhabitants to bear. When the floor of the upstairs room was swept, sand seeped through the gaps, raining down on the occupants below. Many juniors got into trouble for this because the seniors downstairs came back to find sand on their beds, or, in real time, landing on their heads!

That night, sand was the least of our concerns. We would have gladly welcomed heaps of the stuff being shoved through the gaps onto our heads. That scenario was far better than being caught.

We continued to track the flashlight's beam. Eventually, it paused and settled on a small, narrow gap, piercing downwards into our room. Several students shuffled as quietly as they could from the weak rays of the beam. The rays moved to a bigger gap, which forced more of us to shift our positions. The rays stayed fixed on this spot for a long moment. Eventually, they moved away, off the floorboards. Our nemesis could be heard exiting the room upstairs and walking down the hall towards the staircase.

At this point, panic broke out in our room. Had this teacher seen one or some of us through the gaps? Surely, the gap was too narrow. Or had he headed off to check other rooms overhead? What if he were pretending, and summoning reinforcements, because he knew there was a legion of us in my room? Should we bail and get out now? What if there were more teachers around the building?

If the teacher had a monitoring device to track noise levels, he would have concluded that there were students in my room based on the frightened whispers that erupted.

Bang! Bang! Bang!

'Who dey dia? Open di door right now! I be Saul, di commander!'

Game over.

Saul, aka Bentigor, was a borderline-deranged one-man security outfit the school had hired to patrol the campus grounds. A hunter's rifle or *shakabula* was a constant feature on his person, complete with a *Kangol*-styled hat on his head. His presence sent a signal that the school meant business, but looking back, the psychological and mental state of this chap, along with his pervert-like attitude towards the girls, would have led to several lawsuits against the school in other climes.

Bentigor did not have the authority to discipline us, but a drunk security guard holding a gun without a teacher in sight was lord and master at that moment.

'Open di door or I go break am!'

If anyone had a plan B, this was the time to execute it. Escape was top of the list. The collegial spirit that had bound us together before Bentigor found us dissipated quickly. Each to his own.

Most of the rooms in Akinyele House had three windows. The rear windows opened out to a boundary which encircled the building. This boundary was about two metres in width. The soil was completely exposed, deliberately designed to discourage creepy crawlies like snakes and scorpions from getting too close to the building.

The windows had no glass panes. What they did have was cast iron burglary proof in a crisscrossed format. Though sturdy, the lower part of these structures had rusted to expose a gap the size of two rugby balls because lazy students chose to dispose of liquid waste through the windows. There were no sinks in any of our rooms.

No one was bold enough to open the door for Bentigor. Everyone was preoccupied with trying to escape. Whatever plan was hatched would exclude me, because I had a cast on my left leg, having fractured my metatarsals at home during the holidays. Disabled, visibly ill, or those with crutches like me were usually untouchable. So, I knew I simply needed to assume a position on the bed that made my cast visible in order to be spared the wrath of the extremely angry, drunk monster on the other side of the door.

In the two minutes that followed, at least ten students escaped through the gap in the burglary proof, which at first glance looked foreboding. The adrenaline rush overrode any fear that the dangerously jagged metal or the 1.5-metre drop from the window should have struck in the heart of the students.

Bentigor peeked through the windows on the inner-hallway side of the room and realised that the students were slipping away. He scrambled to the rear of the room, but we instantly figured out what he was up to. Somehow, everyone who had escaped through the window managed to evade him. He returned, banging on the door again, threatening to beat the living daylights out of those who remained.

The fact that Bentigor had made the trip to the rear was a problem. Everyone was scared that they could get caught right in the middle of their escape. Unfortunately, there was no other escape route. We were stuck.

We decided that someone had to open the door. The stalemate could not go on forever. A junior tentatively opened the door and was immediately pummelled by Bentigor. Others had positioned themselves around the room, hoping that they would somehow not be detected, or that their punishment would not be as severe. The odds were stacked against them.

Once Bentigor finished battering the junior, he looked around to fish out the other students in what seemed like a hide-and-seek game.

I pleaded the plaster of Paris defense, by showing Bentigor my cast. He ignored me completely, leaving me to spectate.

The obvious next step was to look under each bunk. He dragged Jetta out like a wounded animal and rained blows on him. Yemsta, my junior brother, had chosen to hide under the bunk first. Jetta had followed him. Bentigor did not bother to check whether there was anyone else hiding there once he fished Jetta out, so Yemsta was spared. He knew to keep mute all through the proceedings that followed.

Bentigor decided to take down the names of the students. A few students took their chance and escaped by daring to bolt through the doorway. Jetta was asked to provide the names of everybody who had escaped that evening.

'Dayo Akinsayo, Kunle Teriba, em… Dapo Williams, Idris Kolapo…' He blurted out name after name, hesitating after each.

We listened, wide-eyed, as he invented the names, as Bentigor scrupulously listed each one. His intent was to get Bentigor off our backs, not snitching on the other students. Since Jetta was from Vining House, not Akinyele, he could slip away and find ways to evade Bentigor in the weeks and months to come. If Bentigor ever came back, I would have to find a way to reinforce the truth that there was no Dayo Akinsayo in the room, or Kunle, Dapo, or Idris.

When Bentigor was satisfied, he stumbled through a lecture he felt we needed to hear. Once he finished his rambling, he warned Jetta that all would face the consequences the next day, and walked out, disappearing into the moonless night.

Phew.

We struggled to remember who had been in the room before the raid happened, and how so many escaped before Bentigor came in. Yemsta emerged from hiding first. All through the torture Jetta had endured at the hands of Bentigor, my heart had been in my mouth, fearing he might think to check if anyone else were hiding under the bed. I had sat directly on the bed and shielded Yemsta as much as I could.

'My goodness, talk about an evening!' one of us blurted. 'Did you know—'

'You guys', a voice boomed from a dark corner of the room, startling us, 'how are y'all doin'?'

It was Senior Iddo's voice, a roommate who was repeating the fourth year. Incredibly, all through the interrogation that Bentigor had subjected Jetta to, Senior Iddo had been lying on the upper bed on one of the bunks, completely lifeless – a human chameleon. We were stunned.

The episode with Bentigor had lasted close to thirty minutes. Prep was nearly over, so there was no point leaving the dormitory. Instead, we sat and talked through the incredible experience we had just had. We continued late into the night, after other roommates returned, along with students who happened to wander round 'innocently' to our room.

Bentigor never found Dayo Akinsayo or the others on the list. If he were to conduct a raid like that again, any student caught up in the second episode would have needed to sharpen their evasion skills beyond those displayed by Jetta that night.

As for Bentigor, he may have wondered whether it had all been a dream, since he had been drunk. But then there was the mystery of how that list got into his hands.

***

If Bentigor and Mr Lalupon appear to be one-off extreme cases, let me assure you that it is not so. One of the most notorious teachers who taught Yoruba language beat up a student just because she accidentally stepped on his finely polished shoes. Both Jetta and Sage, my classmates, were flogged on separate occasions by Mr Juyo and Mr Satire respectively. The wounds that resulted from their beatings were so bad they had to leave for home to show their parents who then returned to school with them to have a word with the teachers. There were countless others. And what were the offences? Trespassing, late arrival at assembly, fetching water at the 'wrong' time, walking – instead of running – when a master approached and so on.

In my junior years, my hair was a constant source of harassment from some teachers. The school code for grooming and dressing was strict, but it was nearly impossible to cut one's hair once our parents left us. Both boys and girls were required to have low-cut hair styles, although some latitude was given to girls on the length.

At the end of my first year, just after the school assembly ended, a Physical Education teacher decided to send a strong message to those students whose hair lengths did not comply with the guidelines. He produced a pair of scissors and inspected our hair as we exited the chapel. If he deemed the length excessive, he scissored off enough hair to leave a noticeable gap. I was one of his unfortunate victims.

To this day, it remains a mystery to me why our parents did not properly confront some of our teachers.

When my hair length was not an issue, I still had to contend with certain female teachers who queried my naturally wavy hair. To them, the only explanation for the curls was relaxer cream. Any attempt to explain that their assertion was misplaced was construed as rudeness. Where I could avoid them, I did. Otherwise, I learned to keep my mouth shut and take the rebuke.

One of the most barbaric incidents happened in my third year. A few students had scaled the school fence and somehow made their way to a Federal Government school several kilometres away in Idoani, a town I would later discover I had links to: my paternal grandmother had been captured as a slave there and married off to one of the chiefs in Ilesha, my hometown. The SAJOMACO escapees allegedly went there for a party. The authorities there caught them, brought them back to our school, and delivered them into the hands of our school Principal at the time, whom we had nicknamed Ignominy. He had earned the nickname because he could not give a speech or lecture without using the word.

Ignominy was determined to show that this act of defiance would not be tolerated at SAJOMACO. After flogging the students, he ordered that they be locked in a see-through cage the size of a modern lift, stationed in the dining hall for everyone to see. If ever there was an example that reinforced the view that SAJOMACO was like a prison at times, this was it.

The students spent hours cramped in this cage, and were forced to sleep in it overnight. Luckily for them, the next day was a Saturday, and as luck would have it, it was not any ordinary Saturday. It was visiting day. The students sensed a blockbuster of an afternoon, because we knew a confrontation was inevitable. We could not wait for a parent of one of these kids to show up.

We did not have to wait long. A father arrived before noon. He went completely ballistic.

Ignominy was away from campus that morning. The decision to release the students rested with him, but no one was going to stand in the way of a livid parent. The school authorities produced the keys to the locks in record time and released the students. It beggars belief that any teacher would go to such extremes to punish teenagers. Fortunately, this shameful episode was not repeated during my time at SAJOMACO, and the cage stayed empty afterwards.

Public displays of flogging reached a record high during Ignominy's tenure. There was at least one a week, for a variety of reasons, from mere lateness, or bunking off classes, to the most serious, such as cooking in the dormitories. As the flogging grew, the students began to find ways to rebel. The students being punished tried their best to take the lashings of the cane in style, an attitude that got under the skin of the teachers. Some students padded their buttocks and backs with thick vests or towels. They sometimes knew beforehand that they were going to be flogged at assembly. Soon, the teachers began to check for these paddings.

The toughest students took these beatings without flinching. Six strokes were the minimum. Twelve signalled a major offence. To spite the teachers, the assembly of students would audibly count out the number of the strokes. The higher the count, the louder the students got. It felt like the Colosseum.

The more aggravated the teachers got, the harder the lashes. That produced even more euphoria in the assembly.

Things got to a head when the noise levels reached a crescendo during one of these punishment fests, at which point Ignominy got angry and decided to punish every student.

'Kneel down, raise your hands and close your eyes!'

The lucky students were those in the section of the chapel with concrete flooring. Those in the extension sections knelt on bare soil. The punishment lasted for at least fifteen minutes before we were released.

***

In my second year, a third-year student was caught red-handed by Mr Fado, defecating on a newspaper around one of the extension dormitories. What happened next was hard to comprehend. Mr Fado made the boy walk the entire length of all the classroom blocks on the school grounds while carrying the faeces on the newspaper. The idea was to adopt a shock-and-awe tactic to deter others. His approach made no difference, sadly.

Correcting a teacher, especially in front of the class, was frowned upon. This was an extension of the 'Children should be seen, but not heard' culture. In my first year, my Physical Education teacher was addressing the class on the topic of worms.

'Can anyone give me examples of worms which can cause us illness?' Ms Roti asked.

An uncomfortable silence descended on the class.

'You mean, you children don't know anything about worms?'

It was an uncomfortable subject in some respects, because

some of the examples reminded the students of their own past experiences. Eventually a hand went up.

'Hookworm, ma', one of the girls said.

'Good answer. More examples?'

A boy raised his hand.

'You, yes?'

'Tapeworm'.

'Indeed. See? It's all coming out now. All you pretenders. As if some of you haven't been infected by these things. Don't be shy'.

All this while, I had concealed the fact that my dad was an expert on intestinal worms. I had become desensitised to jars of worms preserved in formaldehyde during my primary school days. After no additional suggestions were forthcoming, I raised my hand.

'Yes, one more. Bunmi, what do you have to add?'

'Ascaris'.

'What? What did you say?'

'Ascaris, ma. It's a type of worm, a roundworm'.

'There's no such thing as that. You're wrong'.

And that was that. There was no such thing as Ascaris. She was the teacher – the one with the final say. The only way this conversation could have been overturned was if another teacher, or someone like my dad, was around to correct Ms Roti. But it was not to be.

Teachers were to be feared and avoided. It took slightly longer for some students to recognise this, especially if they happened to enjoy some preferential treatment from certain teachers. Eventually, they came face to face with this fact.

Sometimes our teachers' true colours were revealed when they surprised us with a cleanliness spot check of our dormitories. Some were brutal, suspending any iota of health and safety to make a point like the decision by a Yoruba language teacher in my second year to ask every student in her class to kneel down under the hot blazing sun at noon for thirty minutes as punishment, despite the risk of heat stroke. So, no surprise that when we had the opportunity to get our own back, some students did not think twice.

For Agriculture class fieldwork, the school required each student to cultivate a row of cassava plants, the health of which was graded at harvest. Our teachers supplied us with the cassava stems to plant. We stuck the stems into the soil and left it to nature to take its course.

Our teachers expected us to look after the plants as they grew, but some students decided not to bother with this process. Instead, around daybreak, on the day of the inspections and grading, they made their way to the farm, looked for healthy cassava plants well away from the student farm plots, and cut a few at the base of the plant. They then stuck these into place in their own plots and hoped for the best.

In one instance, when the teacher grading the plot arrived, after a quick glance down a row of cassava plants, he looked down at his sheet and scribbled a B next to the name of the student who owned the row before moving to the next.

'Whose row is this?'

'Mine, sir', Jelo, one of those who had come early to substitute his with a cut and stake, responded.

'Not bad. How many hours did you spend looking after your cassava?'

'Sir, it took a while *o*. I was here every day, making sure I took out the weeds, but the cassava have turned out very well, so, I'm pleased'.

'You should be pleased'. He turned and looked at us. 'Did the rest of you hear that?' he shouted. 'Every day, he was here, looking after these cassava. This is evidence of sowing and reaping. You can't beat hard work. Never! Or how else do you explain such fine specimen of cassava we are beholding here, *ehn?*'

How else indeed.

My Identity Card

Akinyele House

III

Part Three | Rat Race

'Take courage, my heart: you have been through worse than this. Be strong, saith my heart; I am a soldier; I have seen worse sights than this.'
— Homer

Chapter 11

Love is washing up without being asked is an inscription on a mug my parents had at home. In boarding school, I probably would have changed that definition to *Love is parents showing up on visiting day with the best home-cooked meal and provisions in the right order of priority and proportion.*

Food was important. Period. The worst home-cooked meal was a million times better than the best that boarding school offered.

We were undernourished. This was less evident in first-year students, but when one considers that the meal sizes were exactly the same for every student, despite the five-year age gap between the most senior to the youngest, the oldest students were bound to be hungry most of the time.

It was a typical visiting day during my fourth year. Students were hanging around Akinyele House, receiving and entertaining their families. The structure of the dormitory was such we could see all the hustle and bustle going on in front of the building. A Volkswagen Beetle pulled up. Many of us were on the upper balcony, looking down. The student whose parents had just arrived rushed out and threw himself at them. The joy was palpable.

While making his way across the open area where the cars

were parked to his room, he tripped and emptied some of the food in the bowl he was carrying onto the floor. Given how hungry we were, any home-cooked meal would have been cause for celebration, but this was jollof rice, garnished with chicken, fish, and fried plantain – the gold standard. Given that the garnishing, placed with love and care, constituted the topmost layer in the bowl, pretty much all of it ended up on the floor. A gasp of horror reverberated across Akinyele House.

The student, saddened, trudged away, and we all pitied him. Nobody cleaned up the mess that stared us in the face for the rest of the afternoon. Daylight eventually faded. By the time I left the dormitory for prep, every single bit of chicken, fish, and fried plantain had disappeared. All of it. Many of the students who observed the accident would have predicted that a clean-up, student style, would happen once dusk arrived. It was the SAJOMACO way.

***

A boarding school student would not survive if he or she were allergic to beans, unless such student could afford to buy other types of food from the tuck shop or canteen. This legume was a superfood as far as the school authorities were concerned. Beans were cheaper than most of the other alternatives, like yam, *eba* (derived from cassava), and rice. Usually, the school served our beans in the form of a broth, cooked in tomato and pepper sauce. Sometimes sweetcorn was added. That was it. Nothing else accompanied it. No beef, no chicken, no plantain, no fish. Nothing.

We ate beans practically every day at SAJOMACO. It was

114

simply rotated through the roster. On the very rare occasion that the school found out very late that other foods on the roster were not available, we ended up eating the stuff twice in one day. As much as we despised this mainstay, the impending hunger if we chose to turn up our noses at the food was a greater deterrent. The beans were watery and unhygienic. Bottle-top counters, buttons, pins, stones, and all sorts of organic and inorganic material showed up in our beans. It was not uncommon for a first-year student to find the sight so disgusting that it put him or her off beans, albeit temporarily.

During my fourth year, water was so scarce on campus that the cooks drew water out of a second, alternative reservoir which had been otherwise ignored for years. Despite threatening to stand our ground and refuse to eat because we felt the water was contaminated, we still ate the beans. Our bellies spoke louder than our heads. It wasn't long after the kitchen started to experiment with the water in the second reservoir that another incident happened that epitomised our plight.

'Is it yam they are serving today?' Jetta asked, while a few of us waited in my room for the lunch bell to ring.

'This hunger is doing you plenty *o*', someone replied. 'Didn't we have yam yesterday? We had pap and *akara* for breakfast, and everybody knows it's rice this evening. So, where are you going to fit yam into the three-meals-a-day equation when we haven't had beans yet? Or have you forgotten beans is manna for us?'

'It's the hunger *jare*. Don't mind me'.

Suddenly, Topsy ran into the room. 'Have you heard?'

'Heard what?'

'The kitchen wall – the extension one – has collapsed'.

'Topsy, you and rumour *sha*. Who told you that?' I asked.

'It's not a rumour *o*. Many people are going over to see it. Look!'. He pointed to groups of boys who were heading towards the kitchen.

We all rushed out and joined them. By the time we arrived, we met a crowd and quite some pandemonium. The sight I beheld resembled a bomb site. The entire rear wall had collapsed into the enormous vats being used to cook our beans. We could see the cooks handpicking as much of the rubble and stones they could find out of the vats.

'Why are they trying to pick the stones out of the food?' I overheard a first-year student ask. 'There's no way anybody can eat this. No way. I'm sure the Principal will do something'.

We excused the ignorance of this boy who clearly had a lot to learn about SAJOMACO. There would be no intervention from any teacher or the Principal. The kitchen staff served us the finished product because there was nothing else available. Several students bragged about how there was a line they wouldn't cross with respect to unhygienic food. All that bravado disappeared within an hour when the hunger became unbearable. As much as the food was unsafe and unpleasant to eat, we still ate it, including those students one could have sworn would avoid the beans, like Jelo.

Jelo was arguably the most feared student in my year. He was energetic and strong, and was the fastest over 100 metres in our year. He hated beans. He told us he hadn't cared for them since he was a little boy. So, initially, as a naive first-year student, he gave his plate of beans away. Later, when he had acquired some student wisdom, he sold or traded his beans for another meal, like yam. By our fourth year, not only had Jelo conquered his phobia of beans but he had found ways – sometimes questionable – to beef up his portions.

Cantabing (grabbing extra plates of food), bargaining, doubling, and the outright purchasing of food were the four main ways students increased their food portions. Doubling refers to submitting two or more plates, most likely on two separate tables far from each other to avoid suspicion. Bargaining was effected as trade by barter, or exchanging a meal like beans for another, say, yam, on the same or another day. Rice and bread were the most valuable meals. Students usually exchanged two portions of beans for one portion of bread or rice.

To be flexible, some students sold their meals and chose to spend the proceeds on other food types later, or simply kept the money for other things. Although greed pushed some students to keep selling their meals for money, anorexia or bulimia did not feature in our lives. There was no need for weight control. If anyone had taken our measurements, they would have recommended that we be put on a binge diet.

Submitting more than one plate to the dining hall was very risky. For this reason, juniors rarely engaged in the practice. When a limited number of students submitted more than one plate, the strategy worked for the perpetrators, because the kitchen staff typically incorporated some allowance for a slight excess. Students who got away with this malpractice ended up boasting about it. Greed ensured they pushed the practice to the limit, such that demand, measured by the number of plates submitted, outstripped food supply. The kitchen staff would then be left with no option but to notify the prefects and any interested member of staff.

This put a strain on everyone. What should normally have been a simple dining experience turned into a frustrating, drawn-out, clandestine operation of sheriffs trying to catch robbers by ensuring each student took no more than a single plate of food from the dining hall. At the end of the process, it was logical to conclude that any plate of food left in the hall was a double. If for any reason a student could not make it to the dining hall or was late, the plate's contents would most likely be forfeited and the plate seized or destroyed.

Seniors who forced juniors to submit double plates on their behalf made the lives of juniors miserable whenever the prefects and teachers decided this process of elimination was required to fish out the double plates.

Such was the extent that seniors went to increase their food allocation. Some prefects also became corrupt and turned a blind eye to what was going on. A few even joined in. By my fourth year, the dining hall experience had become, at best, chaotic, at worst, barbaric.

Students would usually congregate around the dining hall as lunch time approached. The normal order of things was for a sufficient number of prefects to arrive before the students were let into the hall. Supervision of the dining hall required a good number of prefects to be present to prevent chaos from ensuing.

Lunch time started to slip. Two o'clock no longer meant 2:00 p.m. Kitchen staff came up with all sorts of stories as to why the delays were happening. We were tired, our energy tanks depleted, and were too hungry to doze off, let alone attempt to study. The hunger pangs became unbearable. On one such day, our collective anger boiled over. Some senior students marched on the dining hall. Without enough prefects to bring them to order, the situation spiralled out of control as they forced their way into the hall. A rush was on.

This scene created the perfect conditions for those who wanted to *cantab* to do so. Two plates were not enough. Some students stole up to five plates and made for the dormitories with their spoils. The fact that several other students would go hungry as a result was inconsequential to them. The situation happened so frequently that we developed a sixth sense for predicting the likelihood of a rush. But our actions were also self-fulfilling: when a student thought a rush was about to take place, he ran towards the dining hall; other students noticed and dashed out of their dormitories. Before long, everyone assumed there was a rush and, by doing so, inadvertently created one, when in fact the first student in the chain could have been running for reasons that had nothing to do with the dining hall. But no one wanted to take any chances when there was the heavy price of an empty stomach to pay if one were proved to be wrong later.

Over time, our seniors took to not only rushing into the dining hall but kicking down the doors until several were destroyed. That made it even easier to launch a rush. There were instances when students rushed the food as it was being wheeled into the hall by kitchen staff. The frightened kitchen ladies got out of the way of the mob as quickly as they could. The situation worsened during the months when final exams were being held, because the dining hall was converted into the exam hall. As a result, we submitted our plates on tables packed far more tightly together. Students had to retrieve their plates and head back into their dormitories to eat, because there was no seating available. This kind of setting made a rush even more likely.

On visiting days, even though families were present and watching in full view, this did not dissuade students from displaying this reprehensible behaviour. The embarrassment was of little consequence to many students whose families couldn't travel down to SAJOMACO because the cost of travel had begun to skyrocket due to Nigeria's economic demise. It was one of the most regrettable and embarrassing periods of our boarding school life.

Chapter 12

Whether in times of plenty or need, there was one food commodity students craved far more than any other. The humble *gari*, or garium sulphate (GaSO$_4$), is the quintessential poor man's food, made from cassava. After slightly fermenting peeled and crushed cassava into a paste, it is roasted until it turns into dry, white, gritty granules. The taste and appearance varies with the quality of the cassava and length of fermentation. Some people add palm oil to give the final product a yellow tint.

Gari ranked higher than any other type of food in a student's life. If presented with a choice of chocolates, biscuits, fine dining, or a bag of *gari* that would last an entire term, any sensible student would pick *gari*. It was a case of long-term gain over any short-term sacrifice.

Gari was special because it packs a punch calorie-wise due to its high starch content. It is very easy to store and can be moved around relatively easily. Its shelf-life is also relatively long – months – long enough for students. However, if the process of making *gari* is rushed, it can lead to food poisoning, even death, because of residual cyanide in the cassava. Given that students didn't make the *gari* on the school campus, there were no major incidences of food poisoning, unlike in places plagued by famine or severe hunger.

Gari is also versatile. It can be prepared with hot water to make *eba* or simply soaked in cold water with sugar and groundnuts (peanuts) as optional, luxurious extras. Since we were not allowed to boil water, we consumed our *gari* cold. Cooked beans and *gari* made a great pairing. Adding *gari* to beans or soaking it in water for a long period of time to allow it to swell creates the illusion that the mixture will be more filling. Even though we were aware of the law of conservation of mass, we preferred the illusion.

We kept the sacks of *gari* we brought to SAJOMACO under lock and key. At the start of term, when lockers were bursting at the seams with all sorts of food and personal care items, space was limited. In addition, to repel insects and vermin, some students placed camphor pellets inside their lockers. No health and safety warning came with these pellets, and no one – not even our parents – advised against putting them close to our food items. It was not unusual to find camphor-flavoured *gari*.

In the first half of term, we were generally well stocked with *gari*. Other food items that were higher in the pecking order, and whose shelf-life could be as low as a few weeks, tended to be consumed first. And because it was poor man's food, theft of *gari* was rare early in any term. By the start of the last month of the term, *gari* would be the last remaining food item. Its availability on campus would nosedive as end of term approached, since it was the obvious solution to every hunger pang.

In the last week of term, juniors could be found roaming around the school grounds with a small cylindrical plastic case. These were recycled containers which would have been

122

used to store spices like curry and thyme previously. The containers were popular because they proved very useful if one were to inadvertently stumble on a supply of *gari*. A full container provided just about enough *gari* to accompany a meal. We nicknamed these containers 'in case of incasity'.

Students were a bit frustrated when their families visited in between visiting days and end of term if the visit was in view of the entire student community. Word would reach other dormitories that the student's *gari* supply had received a boost. A flood of requests would immediately follow, once the parent left the campus. Seniors were particularly insensitive, with the worst of them bullying the juniors into giving them some *gari*.

Towards the end of my second year, Dad and one of his colleagues from OAU, Mr Jegs, paid me a surprise visit. This was a big deal. Not only was this kind of visit rare, especially given how far they had to travel, but it was only a week away from the end of term. My brother Wolex had returned home a few weeks earlier, having completed his third-year exams.

Dad explained that he was passing through Owo to Benin town on a field trip and felt it would be a good idea to stop by. The best thing about this visit was that he brought *gari* with him. But I was a little suspicious. The quantity of *gari* was almost a full term's supply. It felt like a bribe. And from his demeanour, I sensed there was more to this visit.

'I have some news. One is good and one is bad'.

Here we go. I knew this was too good to be true, I thought. 'I guess the good news is that Mum is back from London?'

'Yes, you guessed correctly'.

I reasoned that if Mum were around, that could only mean one thing. I looked at him, apprehensively.

'Mum is around because, well, sadly, Grandma passed away last month'.

I had guessed correctly, but that didn't stop the lightning bolt from jolting my body. Grandma had been there since I knew left from right, good from bad.

It was difficult to process the news. I remembered saying goodbye to her at the start of term, as I left home. She stood in the middle of the road, waving goodbye till I disappeared over the horizon. She must have known.

That image has stuck with me ever since.

'So, when is the burial?' I stammered, doing my best to keep it together.

'Em, the thing is… we buried her three weeks ago'.

I could not believe it. Not only did they keep the news of her death from me but they had already buried her!

'Everybody felt it was better to protect you', my dad explained. 'We didn't want you to be grieving at a time when you were writing your exams'.

After about thirty minutes, Dad and Mr Jegs left.

The news that Mum was back home and I would see her in a week, something that would normally have elated me, was eclipsed by the realisation that I would never see Grandma again – at least in this life. It was hard to take, and completely overshadowed everything that evening. I took some time out, wanting to be left alone. I walked out of my room and stared at the stars above. It was a moonless night.

'God' I whispered, 'I pray that you let me see her one more time. Maybe she can appear once more to me? I've heard stories of this happening to people'.

I needed to express my grief openly, somehow, and about ten minutes of a heart-to-heart with God followed before I made my way back to the dormitory.

My friends consoled me, upon learning of the news, but it wasn't long before attention shifted to the immense quantity of *gari* that Dad had given me.

I easily doled out one of the two bags of *gari* within an hour. Such was the need that I was met with. Days later, when term ended, I had run out, and, ironically, I was forced to ask for handouts from friends with whom I had generously shared my *gari* just days before. Clearly, I struggled with demand–supply management.

Some students felt they could improve on our *gari* situation – that we could do with an upgrade of some sort. The solution was to smuggle raw food onto campus and cook in the dormitories. This was strictly prohibited by the school authorities – and for good reasons too. It was foolhardy to place faith in teenagers when the risk of fire was so high.

The cooking of raw food was a crime that only seniors were willing to undertake. Flouting the rule attracted stiff penalties. In severe cases, a student could be suspended or even expelled. The prohibition did not deter some students from taking the risk, however.

'Raw' was the slang given to any uncooked item – maize, rice, yam, and so on. Of these, the most common food item smuggled onto the campus was rice. Like *gari*, it is easy to store and keep for months. Although not native to the country, Nigerians eat more rice than any other food item.

A boiling ring was the most common equipment used to cook raw. Although there were no sockets on the wall to plug appliances into – deliberately – students found ways around this problem by connecting the boiling ring to the electric cables which dangled from the roof, to which our light bulbs were meant to be connected. Besides a boiling ring, the other option was a charcoal iron. The school kitchen burned logs of wood to cook our food daily, so there was a daily supply of red-hot charcoal. Using a charcoal iron required a certain level of skill. Usually, a first-year student would burn his or her uniform the first time they used these irons, because they lack a thermostat.

Students tried their best to keep their clandestine cooking operations as low key as possible by closing the windows of their rooms, but the aroma always gave them away, especially if they could not resist adding some flavour in the form of stock cubes, or spices.

In an environment where food was generally scarce, starving students could easily detect the whiff of raw being cooked. The combination of the aroma and a setup resembling a drug factory with completely shut windows was even more of a dead giveaway. But it was unusual for students to snitch on each other. So, these cooking operations were rarely reported to the authorities. And because staff passed by the dormitories infrequently, the risk of getting caught was relatively low. This emboldened the offenders.

***

A common tradition that juniors perpetuated almost religiously was a food feast on the final night of term. It was referred to as judgement night, or enjoyment night, even though the former moniker was somewhat baffling.

Enjoyment night was a night picnic. It was a paradox of a sort, because prior to this night, students would have been starving, quite literally. Despite the hunt for *gari* in the weeks

126

prior, some of the most expensive food provisions would have been locked away in storage inside the lockers, destined for this final night. Food in this context meant chocolate powder, powdered milk, biscuits, and margarine. Somehow, a feast was made from these basic food items.

Resisting the temptation to open the packages housing these food items was a real test of will during the term, especially in those final weeks. The madness of enjoyment night became clearer in a student's senior years. A first-year student, however, would rather suffer and starve during the term so it could be on record that he or she participated fully on enjoyment night, based on the kind of spread he or she put on. So seduced were they by the romanticised legend of this special night.

But a binge on the scale that was on show on enjoyment night was bound to have consequences, especially with the students having been on a quasi-forced diet in the weeks leading up to the night. As the body tried to cope with this surge in the intake of chocolate powder and powdered milk, students found themselves having to use the lavatories more often, and this carried on into the first few days of the holidays at home. This did not stop juniors from repeating the same exercise in the terms that followed. The allure of the food fest was too strong.

What was strange about enjoyment night was that juniors even doled out their precious food provisions to seniors who had bullied them during the term. One junior, when I was in my third year, Oppy, decided he had had enough of the seniors always having the upper hand. As with most juniors, he was clueless and naive when he first arrived. I remember him being asked to light a second kerosene lantern in the room.

His lantern was already lit. He looked so bewildered, the rest of us struggled to comprehend what he was processing in his mind. Eventually, we asked him why he was taking so long.

He replied, 'I don't have a matchstick'.

It was hard to contain the laughter that followed, because only a first-year student would miss the fact that the lit lantern was his solution.

But Oppy would wise up over the next few months and get his own back. His brands of food provisions were of the type that made an enjoyment night really special. All through the term, his array of provisions was visible for everyone in the room to behold and salivate over. He stored them in the upper section of his locker. Our seniors teased him all term about his long suffering, trying to encourage him to open these boxes and cans of food. He refused and signalled that he would rather wait till the last night of term.

Enjoyment night eventually came. Even the seniors had resigned themselves to this night, since there was a deadline to the standoff which had played out all term. That evening, Oppy brought out his provisions. But to the shock and horror of the seniors, the entire set was empty. He had consumed the contents throughout the term, right under everyone's noses!

Show me a first-year student who can play food provisions poker with his seniors for a whole term and get the better of them and I'll show you a grown-up junior.

Chapter 13

A few years ago, an acquaintance shared a story with me that captured our parents' obsession with good academic grades.

'You wouldn't believe the regime my dad ran for us when I was young', Seze said.

'I'm sure I'd recognise what you're about to say, because these experiences are common', I responded.

'I know what you mean, but hear me out. While in primary school, a classmate – a boy – finished top of my class in the first term. I can't remember which year exactly'.

'I pity you already. You let the boy beat you?' I cheekily asked. Ignoring me, he carried on.

'My dad decided this was an achievement worth celebrating. I mean the boy's achievement, not mine of course. He then informed the parents of the boy that he would love to take both him and me out for ice cream'.

'Well, this story is definitely better than anything that happened to me. Ice cream? You guys got rewards?' I started to interrogate him.

'Dude, chill… just listen', Seze admonished me. 'My dad spoilt the other boy rotten, buying him whatever he asked for. Me? Well, I got nothing'.

My jaw dropped.

Seze continued. 'My dad told me it was up to me if I wanted a repeat of this experience at the end of the next term. Suffice to say the other boy never claimed the top spot again for the rest of our primary school years. That top spot became the Seze spot'.

'Wow. Well, you definitely deserved the ice cream in the following years. You must have worked really hard'.

Seze laughed hysterically.

'What's so funny?'

'What ice cream?'

'I don't understand'.

'Of course I didn't get any ice cream. Even if I were first out of a thousand students, I wouldn't have gotten the ice cream'.

Being top of the class was the default, expected position – celebrations were for the weaker species who accidentally got to or were allowed to claim the top position because the smarter kids had taken their eyes off the ball.

***

The beginning of my senior secondary school years – that is, my fourth year – could not have been more disruptive. A few days before the term started, I was playing football at home with my brothers. Back then, it did not matter whether it was an actual football. If we found a suitable substitute, we had a game on. And football boots were not necessary. They were a luxury anyway.

On that fateful day, I was playing barefooted. While attempting to take a glorious shot, I ended up kicking a concrete slab, having committed fully to the shot. This miskick brought a swift end to the game as we spent the next two hours massaging my toes with menthol balm. The swelling was so obvious and the pain so excruciating, we had to own up to my dad when he returned home from work.

The next couple of days were frantic. A visit to the hospital confirmed my worst fears: this was no simple injury – I had managed to fracture four metatarsal bones all at once. I would spend the next six weeks in a cast.

Unfortunately for me, we were to resume school the following week. Wolex returned to school as expected, to begin his fifth year, while Yemsta, my younger brother, was scheduled to start his first year slightly later. I stayed back at home with him for the next four weeks. Dad was not sure what to do with me. The fourth year I was about to start was quite an important year, since it was the start of senior school. It was also the first time we were required to specialise in arts or sciences. This was serious stuff.

I had chosen to specialise in sciences. Our year was divided into five arms: classes A through C were for science, while D and E were for art students. Medicine and engineering were the default responses we had been programmed to regurgitate if asked what future career we were interested in. We made allowances for those who wanted to be lawyers or accountants, but anyone with a serious mind chose the A through C classes. Or so we thought.

Because of the stigma associated with the arts at the time, many students who would have flourished had they been allowed to pursue what they were good at ended up going down the wrong path. Although the stereotype is now being challenged, it is hard to dislodge this entrenched view from the Nigerian psyche. Years later, during my A Level and university years, I came to realise Nigerians were not alone in this way of thinking.

Fearing that my long absence from school would have a lasting detrimental impact on my education, four weeks after my injury, Dad decided I should return to school, with my cast still on me, and try to survive somehow. Those weeks I spent at home were not as boring as the eight weeks before I started secondary school almost three years prior. But they were still a slog.

Beyond the initial unwanted attention caused by the cast on my leg, I adapted to school life relatively quickly, with support from my friends, especially Jetta. The sympathy I got from the girls was a bonus. To say the school was supportive would be an exaggeration. Support in this sense was limited to allowing me to pick up my plate of food from the dining hall even if the other students were delayed, and I didn't have to participate in labour activities. Other than that, I was left to my own devices.

Dad returned two weeks later to check up on me at school – and remove the cast. By this time, I had found a way to cope with the major inconvenience that came with the cast, such as not being able to scratch an itch, and the discomfort of wearing a cast in a tropical climate. In fact, on the day Dad returned, I was doing what most boys did – playing football. I could not run, but I was not going to let that stop me. So, I volunteered to be the goalkeeper, a role most Nigerian kids avoid because, everyone wants to show off their dribbling skills. Pelé, Maradona, Okocha, and Kanu were our heroes.

I spotted Dad's car approaching out of the corner of my eye. Somehow, I managed to extract myself from the game; luckily, we had been playing in front of my dormitory. I hobbled along the U-shaped corridor, just in time to evade Dad through the gaps between the pillars until I got to my room.

If I needed a wake-up call that it was back to business as usual when I returned to school, it was the announcement in my first Biology class, the very first week back, that we were to sit a test the following Wednesday. My junior school grades may have been decent, but I was not prepared for any test. Somehow, despite having missed four weeks of classes, I managed to pull off a 78% score when the results came through and also come top of the class.

During the downtime at home after my injury, Dad had shoved a *Modern Biology* textbook into my hands. I think he was biased, being a parasitic worm specialist. By the time I resumed at school, I could draw the nitrogen and carbon cycles from memory. However, before we sat the test, it was clear that the teacher required us to memorise a lot more than we had been used to in our junior years. Even though this was the first term of my senior years, the requirement to memorise a lot of words and diagrams led me to conclude that I was unlikely to pursue certain careers, even Medicine.

In contrast to Biology, I found Chemistry exhilarating. Unfortunately, our Chemistry teachers appeared to struggle with some of the difficult concepts themselves. So, while others devoted themselves to sports, a group of us started a Chemistry knowledge race – to read ahead of class. To read is one thing; to understand is a different kettle of fish. Given that we were racing each other in our knowledge acquisition, no one willingly admitted they struggled with some concepts. There was a lot of grandstanding about how far ahead one had read. In this race, there was only one textbook that mattered: *New School Chemistry* by Osei Yaw Ababio. It was our second Bible.

Before long, we had expanded this knowledge race to other subjects, including my not-so-favourite, Biology. By the end of our first year of senior school, the race which began as a self-serving exercise had become a necessity. Nigeria's political landscape had taken a turn for the worse. The presidential elections of 1993, the year before the start of my senior years, were supposed to usher in a brighter future. The election results were annulled; the winner, M.K.O. Abiola, was jailed and would eventually die in prison under the most suspicious of circumstances six years later.

Nigeria was degenerating right before our very eyes. Not only was the school infrastructure beginning to tear at the seams, but even the committed teachers were having to pick between teaching and looking for other means to feed their families. Industrial action was rife and plagued the rest of our secondary school days.

Shortly after the elections were annulled, on a seemingly normal school day, around midday, word reached my class that a protest march was underway in Owo town, as people spilled onto the streets to challenge the annulment. The march eventually reached our school gate.

SAJOMACO was conveniently situated on the outskirts of Owo town. We had a chip on our shoulders, because we were academically stronger than the other schools in Owo, and we preferred to mind our own business, unless there was some sort of competition that brought the different schools together. Whenever an opportunity to drag SAJOMACO into goings-on in the town arose, the people in the town seized it. This protest was one of such.

The teachers decided to send us to the chapel for our safety, primarily, but they also hoped that they could hide us from the protest, in the event the school gate was breached. Truthfully, the reality was more of a when, not if. Soon, hundreds of agitated protesters – strangers – were crawling all over SAJOMACO grounds. The school authorities were powerless to stop them, and there was no police in sight, because their uniforms made them a target.

The chapel was the only building on campus with a capacity to hold large assemblies comfortably. Anyone with half a brain cell could have figured out where we were hiding. It took less than five minutes for our cover to be blown. A few minutes later we were listening to a man I can only describe as deranged or psychotic. He was mouthing off a lot of garbled nonsense about the elections.

After this uncoordinated mess of a protest subsided, because the protesters tired themselves out and left the campus, we returned to normal school life as though the events of that afternoon had been but a dream.

Looking back, it is difficult to understand why our parents let us remain in school. But what choice did they really have? It felt like everyone in Nigeria was playing a survival game, including our parents.

Given this backdrop, excelling in our academics proved even more important. We became more dedicated to our knowledge race. But soon, a bit of paranoia set in. The objective became how quickly a student could amass enough knowledge to sit the final exams months early, and pass. No one cared much about what the impact could be on the actual progress of a student in other areas, let alone what to do after passing the exams.

I would not fully appreciate the narrowness of the learning methods we were exposed to, or the deficiencies, until I started my A Levels in London a few years later. Two areas where the gaps showed up were in science experiments and our approach to providing answers to questions.

Unlike the final exams held on SAJOMACO campus, those held towards the end of the calendar year at centres outside the school – initially designed for retakes – did not feature practical experiments. Instead, the exams focused on the theories behind the experiments. Preparation for those external exams encouraged us to memorise the results of many of the experiments such that, through a process of elimination, we could work out the correct answers. While this gave us incredible retentive memory, we lacked practical experience. And when we were lucky enough to have the equipment to carry out experiments in school, they were substandard or ancient.

The first time I used a suction device to draw a base solution into a pipette was in my A Level class in London. At SAJOMACO, this was done by mouth. There was no device to help with the suction. We were skilled enough to avoid getting the hazardous solution into our mouths by swapping our lips for our thumbs at the very last second to prevent the liquid from draining quickly back out of the pipette.

At SAJOMACO, we were accustomed to answering exam questions with as many words as possible. A correct answer with no longwinded introduction or extras was unlikely to receive full marks. I realised this burdensome approach had to be dropped during a conversation with my A Level Chemistry teacher.

'Bummy', she began. Mastering the pronunciation of the silent n in my name can be tricky. 'You did rather well in the exercise'.

'Thank you', I replied. 'It wasn't that challenging to be honest. You were nice to us'.

'Yes, yes. It will get more difficult over the coming months. There is one thing though', she continued.

'Hope I haven't made a huge mistake somewhere'.

'No, no, no. How do I say this?'

I wished she just got on with it. This politeness and the roundabout manner through which I was being introduced to English culture was a frustration. Why couldn't she just say what she wanted to say?

'Well, you see here', she said, pointing at the question.

'Yes, the one about photosynthesis. I thought I gave it my best shot. Actually, you gave me full marks too'.

'Yeeeees', she replied, slowly turning her head upwards as she dragged out the word. 'What do you think I might be getting at?'

'Honestly, I don't know. I thought my definition was excellent. It has all the key words in there – process, plants, food, carbon dioxide, etc. I even gave some examples to provide more context'.

'Yes Bummy, you did. All that is fantastic. But it's a one-mark question. One mark'.

This was not the last time I would write an essay-like response to a simple question. After years of indoctrination in an education system that rewarded verbosity, it was a difficult habit to give up.

Career advice at SAJOMACO was largely non-existent. I recall just one of such in my entire time there. And career options were very limited. Broadly speaking, vocations paid well, and were well regarded culturally. Medicine caused the most stress, because many students struggled to get the required grades, even when they were passionate. Many ended up wasting good years pursuing dreams that were dead before they even started, because they were bent on studying the subject. Nothing else would do, not even a derivative in the Health Sciences field.

Chapter 14

Despite the gaps in the accelerated learning we subjected ourselves to, and the harsh conditions we studied under, the benefits outweighed the negatives. During one of my A Level Physics classes in London, Mr Raj, our teacher, decided to do a quick recap on wave properties before moving on to some advanced concepts. We had covered the topic in the prior class. He asked if anyone could give him a simple definition of a wave. He had not provided one in the previous class, but had hoped that it would be a relatively easy question. He was met with stony silence. After a few attempts encouraging us to muster up something – anything – he became a little exasperated.

All through this episode, I had kept quiet, because I was gaining a know-it-all reputation. It was not my fault. I blame SAJOMACO. Eventually, I spoke up.

'A wave is a disturbance which travels through a medium and transfers energy from one point to another without causing any permanent displacement of the medium itself'.

After spending tens of hours at SAJOMACO devouring *Senior Secondary School Physics* by P.N. Okeke, it was inevitable that a definition like this one would become lodged in my brain.

It was not just Physics. In our Maths class, Wolex and I gained a reputation quickly, such that our teachers would only ask us to answer those questions they had already posed to the class which remained unanswered. We were allowed to carry on working on coursework or homework for other subjects to address our boredom. And we also worked on the lesson material for the next class.

'How come you guys enrolled at Barnet instead of Woodhouse?' a friend once asked us. 'That's where the smart people go'.

***

By the start of my fifth year at SAJOMACO, many of my classmates had registered to sit the final exams at other centres far away from school, or closer to home. The opposing argument that we were missing out on school was a weak one, because the brightest students had already covered the topics yet to be taught in class. By the time I started my final year, classes were almost redundant. Not only had we mastered the contents of our curriculum, but we had solved all the questions in our textbooks and were being called on by the teachers to help with questions that other students were having difficulties with. Many of us achieved A grades in those exams we took outside the school, and went on to improve on them in the finals we sat at SAJOMACO a few months later.

It was at the end of my fourth year that the weight of expectations by my family on achieving the best results was revealed. I had managed to achieve A grades in every subject. I couldn't wait to tell my dad. On the last day of term when he showed up, I ran to him and boldly showed him the results.

'I got A in every subject, Dad. Finally!'

He took the report card from me, and gazed at it while walking back to the car.

I was a little bemused, because I didn't understand his need to inspect the details. I already communicated the most important point.

'Hmm, this is fine', he muttered. 'Well done'.

And that was it. That was Dad's response to my Muhammad Ali moment. I finally reached the top and all I got was a 'well done'.

I realised I was probably never going to achieve any academic result that would make my parents – especially Dad – jump out of their chair in excitement. This is the type of family where if you scored 98% in a test, you are asked what happened to the other 2%. I sucked it up and decided I had to just live with it.

I would come to understand that my dad was a super high achiever, whose academic achievements were against much greater odds. But then, it was not just good academic results that we did not celebrate as a family. We were just not very good at throwing parties. I envied friends whose parents threw a proper party for them because they achieved a B.

Standards had slipped since my dad was a student at OAU. Back then, in the '70s, a graduate could secure a place for a Master's or their PhD at Cambridge or Oxford directly, without any fanfare. This contributed to the assumption that we had no option but to be academic geniuses. I recall filling my application form for the university exam to the Joint Admission Matriculation Board, aka JAMB. At the time, my parents hadn't decided to move the family to London. The form allowed me three options for university places. I had some difficulty filling all three in. So, I discussed my dilemma with Dad.

'I know I have to put OAU as my first choice, Dad, but I don't know what to put down for the other two slots. Maybe University of Ibadan? But that's as far as I could go because I really am clueless about the third slot'.

He looked at me like I had just spoken Greek.

'OAU, of course. For all three'.

***

Unlike the brightest students, some students were hell bent on getting good grades but didn't want to put in the required work. As Nigeria slipped into greater malaise, this culture of reaping without sowing escalated. In defence of the school authorities, at least they stood up to the practice of cheating and maintained their integrity. Cheating was not new. Back in my first year, the dominant view that emerged from a conversation with some of my friends was that it was impossible to pass exams in senior years without cheating. This view was based on a statement that one of our seniors had made. Years later, we debunked this view and focused on working hard for our grades. So, we were well aware of the practice; the only difference was that in our senior years, it felt like the practice was on steroids.

What was most disturbing was that students – including the naturally bright ones – were being brainwashed by their seniors into believing that it was impossible to pass or achieve a respectable score in any exam without cheating, or, at the minimum, contemplating the idea of cheating.

Senior Iddo, who was repeating the year during my fourth

year, was a good example of a student who showed promise because of positive peer pressure. He caught the bug for Maths after he started hanging around us. His fortunes began to change and his scores improved. Soon enough, a test came along which wrong-footed him, because the questions were drawn from topics he had not focused on during his revision. Sadly, he never regained the spark he had started to show. Eventually, he got sucked into the world of the cheats. Our worlds grew apart thereafter.

The schemes devised by students to cheat grew ever more elaborate as the years rolled by. Leaks became rampant. A small huddle by students in some backwater dormitory most likely indicated that someone had gotten hold of a leak. The main challenge the students were confronted with was having to memorise the answers, especially if the exam was a multiple choice one, as quickly as possible.

A classic cheating practice utilised a paper label which students slotted inside the transparent tube casing of their BIC ballpoint pens. The label was used to display the name of the owner. Some students began to write answers to questions on the inside face of the labels. Without thoroughly inspecting the pen, teachers were unlikely to foil the deception. Many students got caught while attempting to remove the labels in order to view the answers, but several got away under the noses of unsuspecting invigilators.

Other forms of cheating involved inscribing answers on the inside of the hem of trousers and skirts. The more brazen students sneaked textbooks into the exam hall. Others used toilet breaks to smuggle questions out, or to receive answers. In extreme cases, some students deliberately arrived at the exam late. They would wait for another student to sneak the exam questions out of the hall to them first, hoping to show up at the exam with as many questions as possible answered already.

There were instances when the supposedly sealed exam papers ended up being leaked before the exam – from outside the school. On such days, it was common to find little groups of students in huddles, 'downloading' questions, splitting into teams to work out the answers, and then sharing them. Students would even trade these leaks, offering the questions to others for a fee.

Corruption begets corruption. Sometimes, these leaks were fake. It was unclear whether the exam bodies promoted false leaks, or if some groups and our seniors looked for ways to make a quick buck by profiteering from the scheme. It was extremely satisfying that those who chose not to cheat outperformed the class consistently.

Perhaps this despicable practice would not have gained traction had reporting been actively encouraged. But students rarely broke the unwritten codes of conduct governing student life. Snitching just did not sit well with us. Those who did were ostracised and were likely to become the target of some kind of physical attack.

***

The more diligent some students became, the more narcissistic and hopeless those who struggled, like Senior Iddo, turned. This contributed to the cheating culture of the latter group and helped to create a divide between the cheats and non-cheats, with consequences too.

During a test in my fourth year, my class was being supervised by a youth corper – a university graduate who was serving as a teaching assistant in the compulsory programme which all graduates are expected to participate in. The programme was created in 1973, with the aim of fostering better interaction between the different tribes in Nigeria after the civil war.

Mamuks and I were among the brightest students in my class. After submitting our answer sheets, we left the classroom but stuck around, outside, where we could observe the rest of the class. At some point, we noticed that the corper had placed our answer sheets in a compromising position, deliberately, to allow another student, Eheamey, to view our answers. Eheamey was intelligent, but she seized on the help being offered to her and copied some of our answers. We were livid.

After the test was over and the class dismissed, we confronted her and accused her of cheating. She forcefully rejected our assertions, but onlookers could see that she was lying as she backed away from us, hoping to retreat or escape. We were having none of it. We raised our voices and the argument became agitated. Students like a good argument; a fight is even better. At some point she lashed out at us with her hand. For a bunch of immature teenagers who had been taking karate lessons in their spare time, this was the wrong move by her. We returned fire. *Shoop! Swah! Zonk!* The corper got involved soon after, led us away to a mediation meeting in a quiet office, admitted that he had contributed to what had happened, and apologised. He was protecting his own back, because the consequences would have been grave, had the school authorities found out.

After the adrenaline faded, I regretted that I got into a physical altercation with Eheamey, because it dawned on me that all of us were victims, albeit to different degrees, of this horrible cheating culture.

Two years later, the cheating culture struck again. The night before my Maths finals, several of my friends were in my room, revising, as a group. The pressure was off for most of us, because we had already achieved a pass or distinction in the exams we sat for months prior, outside the school. As such, our revision was quite relaxed. We ended up chatting late into the night and eventually all slept off.

The next morning, I woke up to discover that my scientific solar CASIO calculator had vanished. I cherished this calculator, because it was a unique model. My dad had given one each to Wolex and me a few years back. Despite despatching some juniors to help with a thorough search and reporting the theft to the exam invigilator, since it was logical to expect the calculator to turn up at the exam hall that morning, I never saw the calculator again. And so I sat my Maths finals without my own calculator. I still did well in the exam, thanks to the invigilator being supportive, and allowing the students nearest to me in the hall to lend me their calculators when I needed one.

Chapter 15

A t the time I started at SAJOMACO, although the power supply was epileptic, it was reasonable. Our evening prep classes featured a combination of electric lighting in the classrooms with kerosene lanterns as back-up. A few years later, electric lighting had become a luxury. If a classroom was lucky enough to have power, securing a reading spot was near impossible, because of the overcrowding. Therefore, our kerosene lanterns became indispensable.

As a result of the significance attached to the lanterns, they joined the list of items which brought misery to the life of a junior student. School mirrored the trends in the country at large: the rule of law disintegrated and corruption grew. As death and taxes are certainty to an adult, so was the theft of one's belongings at SAJOMACO. My stolen calculator was the tip of the iceberg. Many a student woke up during prep, having dozed off, to find themselves in pitch darkness. The luckiest ones found their lanterns had simply run out of kerosene. The less lucky ones deduced that their lanterns had been drained of fuel while they slept. The really unlucky ones woke up to find that their lanterns had taken a walk – probably never to be seen again.

Theft was so rampant that kerosene lantern parts, such as the glass casing, even the kerosene tank covers, were stolen. Seniors in my room also capitalised on the rot. They joined a perfected hit-and-run theft of the lanterns – the 'ninja' job. Ninja attire, as the name suggests, referred to the head gear or mask that was made using our school uniform shirts, leaving just the eyes exposed.

One evening, during my fourth year, while we were all in the room relaxing, a ninja burst into the room, picked up the lantern and quickly slammed its base onto the ground, such that the fuel extinguished the flame. This was a half-second job. The room was plunged into darkness and the ninja made off with the lantern. But we were not strangers to this kind of raid, so several of us leapt from our beds and chased after him.

We eventually caught him, but waited for him to reveal his identity. It was too risky to rough him up, because we figured he was most likely a senior, based on his stature.

'You guys were quick *sha'*, he said, as he took off the shirt concealing his face. 'Not bad. At least I know you'll defend our lanterns well, if anyone tries this in the future'.

We were speechless. It was Senior ComCom, one of the seniors in our room.

'You guys know this was a prank, *abi*? I was just testing you', he continued.

'To be honest, we are just still shocked, Senior ComCom', one of the juniors explained, 'because we've heard that this kind of thing happens in some of the other dormitories. They say it's a prank, but every time the prankster isn't caught, you never see the lantern again'.

'Are you saying if you didn't catch up with me, that I'd have stolen the lantern?' an increasingly angry Senior ComCom blurted.

'Em, no…'

'You better watch your mouth. I'm not any rubbish senior'.

Senior ComCom had the last word. We were just grateful that we were able to apprehend him.

After months of low-level lighting with kerosene lanterns, the seniors in my room felt it was time to step up, to upgrade to electric lighting. Senior TaiTai made the case.

'*Eyin* boys, you know we can't be living in darkness. Kerosene lanterns are for *suberus*[4]. We need to be operating at a higher level', he began. '*Shey* you get?'

'Yes, senior', a junior replied.

'So, I want to open the floor to all of you, so that we can all speak our minds', Senior TaiTai said. 'What do you think we should do?'

I spoke first.

'I think we can manage with the kerosene lanterns. I agree that they are not as good as the electric bulbs, but at least they are reliable, unlike NEPA, and…'

'Shut your mouth! You think all of us want to stay in Jurassic Park, like you? Nonsense!'

'I was just trying to—'

'Abeg, keep quiet! Does anyone else have anything to add?'

With no other dissenting voice in the room, we all agreed to purchase a light bulb for the room.

What eventually transpired was a special electric light tax for our room, but one which fell on only the juniors. First, the seniors found a 'fixer' – a student who dared death daily by

---

[4] Dullards.

spending a good portion of his time wading through spaghetti structures of electric cabling in the roof of the thirty-year-plus, not-fit-for-purpose building that we called our dormitory. After paying the fixer to connect our room to the so-called grid in the roof, the seniors organised a bulb for the room. The burden of guarding this light bulb fell on the juniors.

What was not obvious to any outsider was that this electrification of our room was a potential money spinner for our seniors, beyond awarding themselves the initial 'contract'. Within a few days, it was clear what we were up against. One evening, everyone in the room dozed off and forgot to remove the light bulb. Many rooms were not locked overnight, so strangers could wander in. By the morning, the light bulb had disappeared. The seniors cried foul; they had not been in the room the previous evening with the juniors – conveniently.

The replacement cost was another tax the juniors had to bear, never the seniors. Cue round two of the contract tendering process.

'We can't stay in darkness for long, guys. We need a replacement bulb fast. I can't be doing suffer-head. Some of us need to revise. You people need to find another bulb', Senior TaiTai said. 'How much did the last one cost?'

'Five naira'.

'You guys should just divide it amongst yourselves. Make sure you hurry up. I'm expecting the five naira by tomorrow evening'.

'Senior TaiTai, we don't have enough money. We spent most of our pocket money on the last one'.

'Look at this stupid idiot. You think that is my business? Better go and find the five naira. Or you want me to do *were* for you?'

By the evening of the next day, the said five naira appeared, without any contributions from any of the seniors. Senior TaiTai's mood improved as he collected the cash, without batting an eyelid or showing any hint of embarrassment.

In less than thirty minutes, he appeared with a new bulb.

On closer inspection, the rest of the room noticed that the bulb looked a little worn.

'Senior TaiTai, you should return this bulb to the school shop *o*. It looks worn, or even used', a junior commented.

'What do you mean? This is a brand-new bulb. In fact, I was the one that took it out of its packaging just now'.

'It's just that it has scratches on it'.

'So therefore *nko*? Is that proof that it is not new? *Kuwait*[5] out of my face!'

Although Senior TaiTai claimed he had bought a replacement bulb, it was obvious that the bulb was identical to the one that had gone missing, with all the scratch marks that had been put on it deliberately to make it easily identifiable still visible.

Theft was rampant and spread well beyond kerosene lanterns and light bulbs. Charcoal irons were stolen; the charcoal was fair game too. Even electric cables were stolen. Many rooms were not locked, because the locks had been damaged and were never replaced. This meant it was very easy to steal light bulbs. As a result, a custodian was appointed, usually a junior in the room, and assigned to keep the bulbs in his locker. The junior would pay a heavy price if the bulb went missing, or was stolen.

Over time, however, removing the bulbs from their place-

---

[5] SAJOMACO slang meaning 'get out'.

holder sockets was no longer adequate – the sockets and wire too were stolen. The ingenious solution that the students came up with was to cut the wire high up, closer to the ceiling, such that a combination of the wire, socket and bulb became the detachable unit which was then stored away. This new set-up was dangerous, because live wires were left exposed. The students bent the two copper wires from the ceiling to form hooks. They were safety-aware enough to recognise that an insulator had to be put between the two hooks; this insulator was made of foam, most likely from a stolen mattress. This arrangement was very common and in view of all to see when one walked into many rooms. Despite being extremely dangerous, the structure made it easy to simply hang the bulb-wire composite on the double-hook structure dangling from the ceiling. No switch was necessary because the wires were always live.

Unlike the dormitories, our classrooms were lit by fluorescent tubes. Many of the tubes that were supplied when the buildings were first erected were still in use when I started at SAJOMACO. As the years passed, darkness crept into the classrooms because the tubes were either stolen or not replaced when they stopped working. Sometimes, they stopped working because the little glow starter encased in a small cylindrical container became a valuable commodity and was stolen regularly. It was not unusual for groups of students to be found wandering around, looking for anyone – usually a senior – who had a starter, so that they could fire up the fluorescent tube in their class.

Kerosene was a valuable commodity that was kept inside our lockers. But so was the rest of one's belongings. To prevent a thief from taking an interest in one's locker, one needed an imposing lock system or padlock. But during those days of austerity, that was an expensive option. As such, breaking into lockers was a relatively easy job. Even the honest students acquired the skills to break locks very easily – for emergencies, of course. This had become a skillset that was acquired by osmosis, simply by being an observant student.

In my third year, a senior in my room lost his keys. Every student, at some point, has known the horrible feeling that descends on one's life when a key is lost. It turns one's world upside down. It becomes difficult to focus because it is akin to being locked out of one's house.

Apart from our mattresses and school bags, every other item we owned was kept inside our lockers. So began the senior's painful search for his key. The quickest option was to break open the locker and live with the realisation that he would have to leave his locker unlocked for the rest of the term, open to theft. The gamble was painful to watch. Eventually, after about a week, he capitulated. To his horror, upon forcibly opening the locker, he discovered that the most valuable contents – packaged foods – had disappeared.

There was a story told of a junior who washed one of the few items of clothes he had left and hung them to dry outside, on the line. His other clothes had been stolen, despite his initials being sown onto them. He sat, next to the line, waiting for the clothes to dry, but while waiting, he decided to check out a nearby commotion that appeared to be getting out of hand. Although he stepped away for only two minutes, his freshly laundered clothes were no longer hanging on the line by the time he returned.

Chapter 16

During my senior years, the plague of theft got so bad that almost everything that could be stolen was stolen. Buckets and mattresses topped the list. Some students began to padlock their buckets to the bunk beds. It was an effective strategy, because it made it almost impossible to steal the buckets, since the beds would have had to be stolen too. But those who, instead, chose to padlock them to the metal grate under the mattress found that this proved no deterrent. The gratings could be bent out of shape to release the buckets in as little as thirty seconds. In some cases, it was not the buckets that the thieves were after, but the water inside. Whether the bucket was properly secured to the bunk or not, an ingenious thief could empty the water, using a small bowl.

There were even cases of mattresses being stolen while students slept on them! A long, busy day filled with exercise does make for a very sound sleep. Once stolen, the thieves stripped the mattresses bare of their fabric covering. That way, they became indistinguishable from most mattresses on campus.

The risk of theft was the reason why a student's name was tattooed in permanent marker on almost every object a student brought onto campus. Textbooks were easily stolen, so parents made markings of students' names on the side of the books, so that every leaf in the book was marked. Discreet writing of a name on the cover or first page of any book was for the ignorant. The name of the game was to scare away the thieves.

Even mattresses got the marker treatment, with care taken to ensure the ink penetrated the foam in case the cover was stripped off. That did not guarantee the prevention of theft, however, given that the marked bits could easily be torn off. And they were.

I was lucky that one side of my mattress had what could only be described as a baked layer. It was hard, like bread crust. To strip the mattress of the cover and then set to work tearing this crust would have reduced the thickness of the mattress. So, this bought me time and allowed me to reclaim my mattress whenever it was stolen.

Some of the items that were stolen frequently had been provided for free, years earlier, when students arrived in the first year, but the burden was quickly passed on to parents as the economy spiralled downwards. For example, there was enough evidence to show that our library was well kitted out at the outset. Even by the time I first arrived at SAJOMACO, the library functioned relatively well. Within a few years, however, it became less relevant. Books were smuggled out under the noses of the so-called librarians. Crucial pages from books would suddenly go missing, having been ripped out, never to be seen again.

Plates of food were not spared either. But this was not the case early on. In my first year, it was not strange to find plates of food in the dining hall, sometimes having been left untouched for hours. Sometimes it was the food inside the plate that was stolen, and the speed at which this occurred was alarming, in some instances less than ten seconds upon the doors of the dining hall being opened. At other times, it was just the meat that was sitting right on top of the food that had disappeared. By meat, I refer to the tiniest piece of beef that would result in starvation of a toddler, if nothing else accompanied it. The size of this meat was that of the tip of an adult's finger. And 'meat' could mean nothing more than bone, cartilage, tendon, or a lump of fat.

The theft of one's piece of meat, or the entire contents of a plate, was still tolerable. There were other more painful scenarios, such as the disappearance of the plate along with the food. Some students came into the hall with buckets and carted away as many plates of food as their buckets could accommodate.

Before my fifth year, all students were required to submit their plates to the dining hall before the kitchen staff served the food. Unwashed plates were skipped. Once a plate was stolen, the only way to get fed was to find a Good Samaritan who had a spare plate and was happy to lend it out. Pocket monies were not enough as insurance cover. They were meagre. Many students, especially juniors, went days without eating three square meals. And to be clear, this so-called meal was never close to anything resembling a balanced diet. Not only were the portions identical for every student, regardless of age, but over the years, the meal size kept shrinking.

There were rare examples of juniors who later found their lost items. The only problem was that most of the time, these items had made their way into the custody of senior students – shirts being worn, for example. Challenging a senior directly was a high-risk strategy that invariably resulted in a severe beating or some form of punishment. The safest way to recover the clothes was to do a quid pro quo: steal them back.

For our manual labour, we were required to own cutlasses to cut weeds and perform general farm work on campus. It is difficult to adequately capture the turmoil that descended on a student's life if he or she did not possess a cutlass. From time to time, students forgot to bring their cutlasses to school at the start of term. Because their pocket money balances would still have been high at the start of the term, buying a replacement was not a herculean task. Further in the term, however, the theft of one's cutlass represented the onset of misery. A damaged or dull cutlass could trigger a domino effect of cutlass theft. Manual labour would still be apportioned to a student, whether he or she had a cutlass or not. It meant waiting for someone else to finish their labour before the student could borrow one to start their work, something the student knew was destined to be repeated every single day, sometimes more than once a day, until the end of term. Running out of time because a student started cutting grass too late could result in punishment, including forfeiting a meal. There were simply no reliable insurance options.

In my first year, the State Government provided students with desks and chairs. Two years later, a requirement as basic as school furniture had become the responsibility of the students and their parents. Standards were tumbling, so it was not surprising that what some students could afford was of inferior quality. Sometimes the chairs and desks did not last a full school year. It was possible to get by without a chair during lectures, but this proved impossible during exam periods. During those times, chair theft spiked.

Similarly, the assembly hall did not have enough benches. Those who could not get a seat were forced to stand. However, there were occasions when the school allowed chairs to be taken from classes to the assembly hall, say, for a church service, or an event scheduled to last more than an hour. These events provided the best cover for chair thieves, because of the chaos they created, since chairs were not sourced or arranged in an orderly manner. It was a race against time to find one's chair before exams started. And if one failed at this task, the only option was to 'borrow', indefinitely, another chair whose owner had not yet claimed it, until one's own chair was found.

Even the kitchen staff got involved in the act, stealing from the food store. Soon, the school made it mandatory that security personnel check their bags on their way out of the school every day. Some were caught and dismissed, but the gravy train may have served several corrupt kitchen staff for years.

Although no academic staff was ever caught stealing, some engaged in questionable practices. One related to the school emblem on our uniforms. Parents were required to source the material from which our uniforms were made, by themselves, away from school. The process was not standardised. Picking the correct shade of brown or blue was guesswork at best. But if the colours did not deviate significantly, one was safe.

For the badge, however, there was a centralised process: the school supplied them. In my third year, a new senior staff member, KwaKwa, was appointed. Not long after he arrived, the badge depository and 'contract' somehow ended up with him and his wife. We probably wouldn't have cared much where our badges came from, but the couple were among the most hated on campus because they were quick to flog students for even minor offences, and many students alleged that they inflated the price of the badge. Inexplicably, the school authorities never investigated, talk less of raising an objection. Instead, they chose to harass us when we tried to do our best to make it through a term without a badge on our uniforms. The cat and mouse game with the students became tiring even for the school authorities, eventually. In time, we settled on a fragile ceasefire which made badge wearing optional – unofficially.

***

Sometimes students felt justified in stealing school property because of the conditions we were subjected to. And I am not referring to corporal punishment. That remains a standard, acceptable way of life that is probably never going to change. Parents who kicked up a fuss about corporal punishment were seen by both students and staff as soft. Any reasonable society would shriek in horror at the experiences we had at SAJOMACO, and call some of the practices what they really were – child labour. The fact is that there are cultural reasons why some of these practices were not even frowned upon. In the same vein, many students wouldn't think twice about stealing from the school farm.

Agriculture remains a big part of Nigerian life. The country is blessed with some of the most fertile land in Africa. It features strongly in the school curriculum, both the theoretical and practical aspects. Cutlasses and hoes were standard requirements for all students. There was no sex discrimination here, either. Boys seized the opportunity to impress the girls, since farm work sometimes meant everyone was together.

After seemingly endless weeks of toiling, harvest time made one feel that all the hard work one had put in on the farm had been worth it. However, although maize and root crops such as cassava and yam are staples with respect to the Nigerian diet, the crop most favoured by our teachers was soybeans. A soybean harvest was a proper jamboree in school. The students had to get on with harvesting the crop, because the teachers would usually turn out in full force to supervise the work. Once the harvest was gathered, a meaningful portion of it was shared amongst the teachers, while the rest was sold on behalf of the school.

Students always felt they got a raw deal as far as this arrangement was concerned. We were not keen on this crop at all. Maize was our preferred crop, because it could easily be harvested from the farms and consumed with very little effort. There were times when this resentment led to students taking the most brazen of risks, sometimes laced with an unimaginable dose of idiocy, like was on display when a student in my year, Oyinbo, decided to raid a maize plantation.

Most plantations were located behind our classrooms such that someone looking on from the dormitories was unlikely to see anyone on the farm. The stupidity behind Oyinbo's plan was multi-layered. For starters, he carried out his raid during the first lesson period, when students were in class. Even though he was at least two hundred metres from our class, it was easy to spot anyone walking through the farm. Had this been any regular student, he might have gotten away with the raid, except that in Oyinbo's case, even a bat could tell that it was him: he was the only albino on campus, hence his nickname. Oyinbo loosely translates as 'white person'.

While some students chose to vent their frustrations by attacking a maize plantation, some bolder students decided to take the fight to the teachers, or, in a sense, give the teachers some payback. These students were typically from the notorious Lennon House. Their reputation preceded them. Staff living close to the boys' dormitories were the most at risk. If chicken from a staff's poultry were to wander too far from the staff's compound, they often disappeared mysteriously. The disappearance tended to coincide later with whispers that the boys' dormitory had enjoyed a feast of grilled chicken that same night.

There was one incident involving the theft of food items from the school store. We were woken up abruptly on a Sunday morning and asked to congregate in front of the store. We were told that the thief had absconded with some yam tubers, amongst other things. The culprit was never found, but the Lennon House boys were regarded as the most likely suspects. Others claimed to have seen several strangers wandering around the school grounds that morning.

During my fifth year, along with some of my other class-mates, I was supervising harvest work being carried out by some juniors on the same maize plantation Oyinbo had targeted years earlier. We had the luxury of sitting under the shade, in the corridor outside the classroom block, which overlooked the plantation. Sadly for those juniors, they got the wrong set of supervisors that day. Some of us decided to take a walk through the farm. Having walked this road before, we knew what students were capable of. It wasn't long before we discovered an almighty stash of corn hidden inside an undergrowth. No one could explain how these juicy looking corns made their way to a spot that ensured they were hidden from untrained eyes. Since no one put themselves forward to claim them, we took custody of them for the school.

Such is life.

Chapter 17

The environment we persevered through could not have been more disruptive during our final years in school. Our parents also never fully appreciated the risks they took by sending us far away from home. How no one died accidentally remains a mystery to this day.

Nothing drew out the risk-taking behaviour in students more than food. Mango trees were the most common fruit trees on the school grounds. Unlike crops that we grew on the farms, the school had a flexible policy towards the plucking of fruits. However, the closer the trees were to the houses of our teachers or the staff administration office, the less lenient the teachers were, especially if they were newly employed. Watching ripened fruits rot when we were hungry was torturous. So, we grew careless of the consequences of stepping on any teacher's toes.

The mango harvest season lasts for around three months, from late February to May. Usually, the rains do not show up till April. If the start of the rainy season coincided with the mango harvest, the downpour did some of the hard work for us. Most of the time, however, students ended up harvesting the fruits manually. The harvesting was sometimes so frenzied that up to twenty students could be found under the tree at any given time. In order to get their hands on the mangoes, students launched all sorts of missiles at the trees. Wooden bits from damaged furniture, metal rods, and stones were the most common, in that order. Not only was the risk of a serious physical injury an ever-present danger, but the mangoes, themselves, carried their own risk. This was mainly because patience was not really a student virtue. At least half of the mangoes plucked and eaten were not ripe. Many students ended up with stomach upsets. And in an environment where milk of magnesia was scarce, we simply endured the pain till it passed. By the time the students reached their senior years, they would have mastered the art of participating in this dangerous exercise without getting injured while their bodies adjusted to eating partially ripened mangoes.

Besides mangoes, students took risks with other fruits, like coconuts. Though common in the markets, coconuts were difficult to harvest, even for adults. At SAJOMACO, hunger pangs forced students to harvest them before they had ripened properly. Coconuts complemented *gari* and beans very well. If purchased from the market, they would have had their husks removed, a fairly difficult and dangerous task, as a sharp cutlass and great skill were needed to do the job.

Despite the abundance of coconut trees on campus, there was some knowledge about the fruit we did not pick up while at SAJOMACO. For example, none of us realised that one of the holes at the top of the coconut is soft enough to burrow into with something hard, like the handle of a spoon or fork, in order to drain the water out, without having to crack open the coconut itself.

Other fruits we became acquainted with included palm kernels and cashew nuts. The former was purely out of desperation because there was very little to extract from these tiny fruits. Cashews, on the other hand, were a revelation. We learned the hard way that the juicy part had to be treated with respect, because it was almost impossible to get rid of the stain if the liquid were to get onto one's clothes. As for the hardened bit, we enjoyed the process of collecting several of these, drying them, roasting them in the embers in the kitchen – if we were ever allowed, or managed to access the fireplace without being detected – and extracting the nuts later. Our parents were surprised when we returned home and began foraging around the neighbourhood for fruits that we would normally have ignored. SAJOMACO had definitely opened our eyes.

As for our actual school meals, it was very common for a junior to borrow a plate from a friend because a senior had started to make life hell for him or her. Sometimes, the junior needed to borrow the plate in order to submit an extra plate for a senior illegally, because the latter demanded it. Worse, the senior may have seized the junior's own plate. Wolex and I were known to have extra plates in our lockers. So, we were on the other side of these requests occasionally.

On one such occasion, a friend asked me to lend him an extra plate. I realised that I had grown more than a backbone when I reflected on the request and refused to lend him the extra plate I had. As much as I could see the need, I justified my position by pointing out that if my own plate were stolen or damaged, or for whatever reason I had no access to it any longer, if I lent out the spare, I might not be able to retrieve it, especially if it entered the control sphere of a senior.

On another occasion, my friend Rex was down with malaria. The seniors in his room sent word out, in case any of his friends had antimalarial tablets. Eventually, the request got to me. Being the children of a nurse and a parasitologist, Wolex and I were mini-chemists on campus, with more than your standard first-aid kits. I had enough malaria tablets for one dose of treatment. Again, similar to the request for a spare plate, I refused to give out my tablets, because I reasoned that the clinic should shoulder this problem, and, more importantly, I shuddered at the thought of succumbing to malaria later in the term when I had no tablets left. The default chloroquine treatment by the school clinic was not a prospect I was willing to face because of the side effects, of which itching was the worst.

There were times when mercy triumphed over logic, though. Just over a week before the end of the second term in my fourth year, I had given out the last of my malaria tablets only to succumb to malaria myself the following week. My preference was to somehow survive to the end of term and be treated at home, instead of going to the school clinic. This meant I turned my attention to treating my symptoms, instead of the underlying malaria. I had just enough paracetamol tablets left to last me till the end of term. So, I would take the tablets once my fever became unbearable. At the time, I did not realise just how dangerous this approach was. The malaria would most likely have killed me, had the parasite succeeded in reaching my brain.

Many students experienced for the first time what an electric shock felt like at SAJOMACO by holding onto metal posts outside the newer dormitories. Virtually nothing was done to address the issue. The other dormitories were not very safe either, even if they carried little electrocution risk. Akinyele House, my dormitory, was a sprawling mansion-like structure with twenty-eight rooms and four large communal rooms, split equally between the ground floor and the first floor. None of the first-floor rooms had any kind of burglary proofing, despite the steep drop from the rear windows. These first-floor rooms aren't remembered for the risk they posed but for the pranks students played. Occasionally, students on the ground floor were showered with waste water by students on the first floor who were too lazy to wash their plates on the ground floor, or who felt it was too much trouble to make their way down the stairs to dispose of the water. The worst examples involved students urinating from the first floor, sometimes intentionally, at other times while sleepwalking, directly onto the ground below, at night.

The electrification of Akinyele House appeared to have been a later addition, after the building was completed, because the state of the electric cables which crisscrossed the roof would give a safety inspector a heart attack. Daredevil students, or self-anointed electricians, who stepped in to make a quick buck, risked the lives of many. Worse still, the cables these mavericks brought into school to carry out their so-called repair work were of such low quality that the spontaneous melting of copper cables became a regular occurrence.

It was nothing short of a miracle that the hatchet job the students carried out did not result in the entire buildings burning down. But we did have some major fires. A section of our chapel burned down during my time at SAJOMACO. The source of the fire was never ascertained, but the most likely cause was faulty wiring.

The infrastructure around the campus was bad enough, but in the way life was lived on campus, it felt like we regularly sought out danger. Students often played a prank involving small fireworks, the size of candlesticks. Pranksters would sail by a room and launch them inside. The more packed the room was with students, the better.

I once witnessed such an assault on a room. The fireworks landed on a bed. In the panic that ensued, a student on the bed got entangled with the fireworks while trapped inside a mosquito net, before the fireworks went off with a bang. The student escaped with only minor injuries, thankfully.

There were other near-death experiences, close shaves, and serious injuries. Senseless arguments broke out over the most inconsequential stories. There were rumours and counter-rumours, neither of which anyone could prove or disprove. When the conversations got really heated, fights broke out. Some seniors acquired their infamy by way of such fights. Waiting in the wings were new challengers who hoped to pick a fight with the established names, as a rite of passage. The more desperate these challengers became, the more ridiculous things they did to show off. In one of the extension dormitories, two seniors started a fight. Compared with the older student dormitories, these extension buildings were relatively modern, complete with glass louvre blades. Instead of fighting with sticks or leftover wooden parts of damaged furniture, as was customary, the students opted for the louvre blades. And one blade was not enough. Several were broken with their bare hands. They then launched the broken panes at each other. While all this was going on, other students stood, gesticulating, cheering them on, ignoring the risk that one of those panes could fly towards them.

While most students avoided taking part in senseless fights, we all shared in the universal struggle to find water. In my first year, the availability of water was a big factor in my parents' decision to pick SAJOMACO amongst the Ondo State unity schools. Unfortunately, in my final years, the same could not be said about the school.

Between Akinyele House and the dining hall stood two huge water reservoirs. In my first year, one of these reservoirs would regularly overflow, because there was no stop mechanism to regulate it once it was full. The water overflowed into the drain and ran all the way down towards the school gate. We got used to this sight. Apart from the fact that the second reservoir was surplus to requirement in a way, there were rumours that many years prior, a student had died in it, arguably nothing more than a legend that had been passed down over the years.

During those years when the main reservoir functioned well, most students preferred to fill their buckets from the tap, which was situated at the very top of the reservoir and connected to the main line from the water corporation, rather than draw from the water stored inside it. We had zero tolerance for contaminated water at that time. When the water corporation did not pump water to the school, we simply waited. Initially, the wait lasted no more than a few hours to a day or two. Within two years after I started at SAJOMACO however, water supply became so unreliable that, in my final year, the taps were dry most of the time.

In its heyday, the reservoir supplied the boys' dormitories and the kitchen with enough water all year round. The girls' dormitories were served by water tanks, not like our reservoirs. From time to time, the girls descended on the boys' reservoirs and drained our supply. Although we saw them as a nuisance when they showed up, we were accommodating. In truth, we did not have a choice.

The busiest period for drawing water from the reservoir was usually around 6:00 a.m., when students were rushing to bathe. At its peak, up to thirty students could be on top of the reservoir, trying to draw water from an opening less than half a square metre in area. As the level of the water dropped, we devised clever ways to draw water. Lying face down only got us so far. We did not come to boarding school with pitchers used to draw water from wells in many homes; these had long ropes tied to them. Instead, we ended up using our belts, which we tied to the handle of our buckets. Unfortunately, these belts were often not strong enough and snapped eventually. And that meant saying goodbye to one's bucket. Sometimes, the buckets fell into the reservoir because the water level was beyond reach, or we had tried to do the impossible by straining too much. Although no one fell into the reservoir during my time at SAJOMACO, a few students had close encounters, including Danksy, a friend, in our first year.

It was painful to watch one's bucket gradually take in water once it fell in, until it was completely submerged and descend into the dark bowels of the reservoir. The loss of a bucket was very unfortunate, because it turned one into a beggar, a second-class citizen who had to depend on other students for water all of the time. But what was a loss to a student, especially a junior, was a golden opportunity for another, usually a senior. The more buckets that fell into the reservoir, the more some students realised they could make some quick cash by conducting rescue operations.

The opportunists returned to school after the holidays with a hook-rope combination. They waited for periods when students were idle or waiting for the dining bell to ring to maximise the visibility of their operation. Rescuing a bucket from the reservoir was down to luck. Notwithstanding, many buckets were brought back to the surface. The rescuer would then charge a release fee. Being reunited with one's bucket took a huge burden off one's life. It was pure relief. But the resurrected buckets that had spent weeks, or months, in the reservoir emerged as a shadow of their former selves, caked in mud. Sand was usually the best cleaning agent. The state of rescued buckets showed just how unhygienic the reservoir was. At best, the health-conscious students would use a disinfectant during the clean-up. Most students were just grateful to be reunited with their buckets.

Sometimes, students were so unlucky that they missed the timing of the rescue operation. Their buckets quickly disappeared, sold to the highest bidder. The original owners would chase shadows based on hearsay or, if they were lucky, credible evidence. In my third year, a friend told me he had seen my bucket in Owo town, in a house situated within a short distance of the school gates. Luckily, half term was close. I was fortunate to retrieve the bucket.

As the water supply from the water corporation reduced over the years, the reservoir eventually dried up. The shortage of water disrupted both student life and the school's activities to such a point that water had to be supplied from outside the school to cook our meals. At its worst, we ended up leaving the school grounds en masse, wandering around Owo town looking for water. The town was suffering too, but not as much as we were. The lucky amongst us filled their buckets before the town folk shut off their own supplies. We then had to trek, sometimes for hours, buckets on heads, back to school. SAJOMACO students once ended up in a big fight with students of a nearby school, Owo High School, because they had strayed, like cattle, onto the other school's grounds while searching for water. Another group of students was attacked by a swarm of bees. Guarding one's bucket of water took on a whole new level of significance during this period.

Chapter 18

The 1990s were a time of austerity in Nigeria. Though not evident when I started school, government reforms gathered pace in the following two years. Along with SAP (structural adjustment programme), other reform-related acronyms, initialisms, and phrases, such as DFFRI, MAMSER, and BETTER LIFE, came to dominate our vocabulary. None of these programmes had any lasting impact on our lives, sadly. They represent vehicles through which substandard infrastructure was constructed and white elephant projects were set in motion. In the process, vast amounts of money were wasted or embezzled.

The reform initiatives were usually introduced with much fanfare and optimism. A well was dug next to our dining hall and connected to an overhead tank with 'Directorate of Foods, Road and Rural Infrastructure (DFFRI)' emblazoned on it for all to see. At the onset, only one of the three taps below the tank worked properly. Within a year, the mechanism to pump water into the tank had failed. Thankfully, the well did not dry up quickly. Up until this point, we found wells intriguing, because the sight that confronted one when staring down the huge dark hole was terrifying. Wells were scary, and demanded respect. At least that was how it felt to some of us who were not used to drawing water from wells at home.

All that mystique disappeared very quickly. Students attacked wells with such ferocity, draining the water more quickly than the ground could replenish. Once we descended on a well, we had to wait patiently while our makeshift pitchers filled. When the pitchers broke free from the ropes they were secured with, we climbed into the wells. There were footholds for emergencies: to our minds, our need to enter the well qualified as an emergency. When we got more desperate, we devised a system in which a few students would stand at various levels of the cross-section of the well, using the small footholds as support. The student at the bottom of the well would fill a bucket or pitcher with water and pass it up the human chain. As far as we were concerned, this was a much more efficient way of drawing water. Our parents would have no doubt seen things differently.

Upon returning home, our house help, 'Aunty' Victoria, was absolutely shocked to find that we were fearless about entering the deep well that had been dug recently, at the rear of our compound. Before then, the well was rarely opened, because water was pumped into an overhead tank regularly. My dad could not believe his ears when he discovered what we had been up to.

The more daring we became at fetching water from wells, the scarcer water became on campus. Sourcing water became a major preoccupation for us. Students started to miss classes. Morale dipped because staff were also fighting their own water demons at home.

As the situation deteriorated, the school authorities encouraged and organised what seemed like an expedition to return to old, abandoned wells that dotted areas of the school we hadn't explored. Tales of lost wells were resurrected, and through collective memory, the wells, overgrown with bushes, were tracked down. A few were located around the girls' dormitories. Within a few days, however, they, too, were bled dry.

We moved on to looking for fresh water beyond the school farms. Anything would do. Flood plains, creeks, streams. Bamboo plants were a good indicator that water sources were near. When the streams proved very shallow, we would use our bare hands to create makeshift waterholes, removing as much sand as possible to allow water to seep into the holes we dug. Once the holes were wide enough, we would let them rest, returning several hours later to find enough water to fill up to ten buckets. But the water was naturally very muddy. So, a long period of waiting patiently for sedimentation to take its course would follow. Some of the water holes we dug became breeding grounds for mosquitoes. However, our desperation for water meant that we simply scooped the larvae off the surface, or removed whatever had found its way into our holes, before filling our buckets.

To beat the rush hour for water in the mornings, students got up as early as 4:00 a.m. and made their way through the farms and bushes to streams, creeks, and waterholes. The lucky ones had flashlights and kerosene lanterns; yet, even these students were taking huge risks just to fetch water.

The girls were usually under more pressure than the boys for water needs. They used more water than the average boy and looked for water round the clock. As much as we thought they were a nuisance when they strayed into the boys' dormitory area to draw from our reservoir, a few boys had sisters on campus, making it difficult to be apathetic or dismissive of them. It was often said that at every hour of the day, if one ventured into the dark crevices of the school grounds looking for water, one was guaranteed to come across a group of female students – usually juniors – on the water trail.

Except for our seniors, drought forced a change in how we thought about conserving water like no other phenomenon. Some of them still demanded their two buckets to bathe. For the rest of us, mere mortals, we mastered the art of sharing a bucket of water amongst up to four people, even when we used soap. Necessity really is the mother of invention. Washing our clothes also required new methods and skills. Instead of dipping the clothes in a bucket of soapy water, we learned to dab the dirty patches with just the right amount of water and soap required to wash. Rinsing off the soap was a staged process, using the tiniest amount of water at each stage and the most extreme form of recycling known to man.

The combination of the last few weeks of term and water scarcity made life extremely painful. It was one thing to be deprived of water for bathing and washing; it was quite another to find oneself struggling to find potable water to drink. Worse still, end of term added to our misery because food, particularly *gari*, was hard to come by. In my second year, during one of these end-of-term periods, my friend Tee had been wandering the school grounds, looking for *gari*. After a generous soul gave him some, he moved on to search for water. This search lasted more than two hours into early evening. As the sun set and darkness fell, students made their way to prep, a pointless exercise at the time, given that we had finished our exams. Tee stayed behind a little longer, hoping to get lucky with his water search. He made his way to one of the extension dormitories behind Okusanya House. To his amazement, he found a keg of water sitting on the windowsill. This was too good to be true, he thought.

By this time, the dormitory was almost empty. Normally, he would shout out to ask if anybody owned the keg of water and ask if they could give him some to soak his *gari*. Even if just from a health and safety standpoint, it made sense to ask for the owner. But what if the owner of the keg proved difficult and refused?

He decided he couldn't risk the owner refusing him some. So, he went in for the kill and filled his cup to the brim. While the darkness provided the perfect cover for this operation, it also made it a tad difficult to see what he was doing. Once satisfied, he stealthily made his way out and sped back to his dormitory. His face brimming with joy, he added two cubes of sugar he had secured from a friend earlier that day. His *gari* was perfect now – and his hunger made it even more tantalising. As he put his spoon into the cup, he kept pondering why it had been so easy to find water in the dormitory. This was like gold after all; it should not have been that easy.

He banished those thoughts and set his mind on enjoying this rare delightful treat. He lifted the first spoon out of the cup. That spoonful would be the last. As the *gari* made contact with his taste buds, he reflexively spat the entire contents out in disgust, and spent the next hour spitting, ever more desperate for water, trying to get rid of any remaining residue. Tee learned the harsh lesson others had learned the hard way: a keg of water lying unclaimed in an open dormitory when water was scarce was akin to a false positive. The liquid was more likely to be kerosene.

***

When scarcity of water, food, and *gari* had taken their toll, and we had been defeated in our quest for sustenance such that we had no option left but to wait for the dining hall bell to ring, life turned into a 'to each his own' existence. Sometimes sports filled this void; for some, it was arts and craft, while others threw themselves into religious activities. Storytellers shone during these periods, narrating entire movies from beginning to end.

Games were also popular. In my fourth year, PRIMEFAC-TOR swept through campus. This was a quiz requiring players to give examples of, say, capital cities in the world. A pause or a wrong or repeated answer would earn the erring player a P, then R, and so on until the player reached the final R of the game's name, at which point he was out.

On the day term ended, the adrenaline rush we felt was a boost. If the value of water and *gari* peaked in the last week of term, it plummeted on the final day. In fact, several students did not bother to visit the dining hall. It was the ultimate symbolic turning up of one's nose to show that this slavery, this oppression, this reduction of our humanity to its most basic form of food and water, had ended. The cycle would undoubtedly be repeated the following term, with all of the pain that came with being a student at SAJOMACO, but for those brief moments, we were survivors, heading into an even more glorious period of holidays – and freedom!

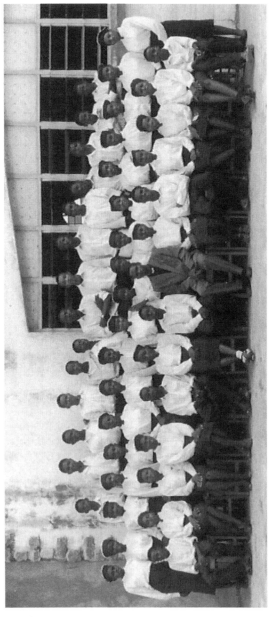

Choir (1995): front row, five from the right (me); back row, two from the right (Yemsta)

IV

Part Four | Poisoned Chalice

*'Men are so quick to blame the gods: they say that we
devise their misery. But they
themselves- in their depravity- design
grief greater than the griefs that fate assigns.'*
— *Homer*

Chapter 19

From the moment the reality of boarding school experience dawns on a first-year student, he or she longs for graduation day – to be free to walk in and out of campus, at will.

Senior years promised us a lot more freedom than our junior years had. Amongst other things, they allowed us to maximise the time we spent on our hobbies. I joined the choir, the Christian drama group, formed a band and wrote several songs. Some of the songs became so popular that the lyrics featured in school prayers. It was satisfying to hear a girl humming one of these songs while she was sweeping a classroom floor. I had written the song a few days earlier and sung it at the Sunday service.

In my senior years, occasionally I travelled with the choir to the state capital, Akure, to sing at various functions at the Ondo State Government House, and other times for quiz competitions which were broadcast on state television. The allowance we were given was entangled in bureaucracy because there were several layers of administrative officers between the finance ministry of the state government and us. Some students alleged that what reached us was a fraction of what was disbursed because everyone believed the middlemen would have creamed off a slice of the initial sum. Such was the strength of the feeling about how engrained corruption was in the system. But something is better than nothing, we reasoned. And we were simply happy to have a valid reason for leaving school for something more exciting than SAJOMACO on those days.

Although we wouldn't experience true freedom until our final-year exams were out of the way, a gradual shift had been happening over the years. We saw a glimpse of this freedom in the second year because as second-year students, we were not at the bottom of the totem pole anymore. Our fifth year provided the best opportunity to maximise the freedom we looked forward to. By then, Wolex and his classmates who were then in their sixth year, though still around on campus, were a shadow of themselves, because their priorities had shifted to their final-year exams. For my year group, it felt like a coronation was truly underway, to make us the rightful rulers on campus.

That said, the senior years were not without their challenges. They forced us to grow up quickly and take much more responsibility for our actions. We couldn't blame someone else for things that did not go our way. Embarrassing habits like bedwetting became less tolerable, because more juniors were around, watching us.

There were some surprises, and unintended consequences, of moving through the senior years. Once the sixth-year students vacated the campus and it dawned on fifth-year students that they had now risen to the top of the food chain, extreme behaviours emerged. Some students decided that it was now their turn to oppress other students, despite having complained about the unfair treatment they had, themselves, received during their junior years.

Thankfully, not everyone behaved this badly. Samba was a good friend who was built more like a bouncer at a nightclub than a student. He got into a lot of trouble in our first year because he was a magnet for conflict. Despite his giant stature, he set a good example by choosing to run the most laborious errands, such as fetching water, by himself for the first-year students in his room. Once, during a rush on the dining hall, he muscled his way into the crowd to free another classmate who was being crushed by the weight of the crowd and was at risk of suffocating. For the likes of Samba, it was clear that the freedom we enjoyed in later years allowed his virtues to bloom.

As the fifth-year students awakened to their new dominance, the sixth-year students grappled with the transient nature of their final year. That fragility, combined with the daunting prospects of an unknown world outside the school gates, evoked emotions in even the most stoic of seniors. It was during this transition period that some of the most trouble-some seniors started to reveal that they had a heart. Attitudes changed; charity and benevolence blossomed.

One of the most difficult year groups I encountered on campus was the one that was two years ahead of mine. This was the year group that Baji, the senior who forced me to become his personal errand boy during my fourth year, belonged to. He was the most imposing student of that cohort. Although he was not a horrible senior, most students feared him because of his physique. There were hints, however, from time to time, that he did have a soul. Occasionally, he would choose to forgo his dinner and let me have it. But he was no softie. He demanded complete loyalty and obedience –

no discussion, no pushback, no opportunity to decline. His reputation went before him as being a no-nonsense character. Everyone knew.

The night before Baji's year group left the school for good, the school organised a proper send-off event. The teachers and the students put aside their differences. The event was held in the boys' dining hall. It was the first of its kind in my time at SAJOMACO, a school-wide event in the boys' section of the school grounds with girls also attending. Baji was permitted to address the school. After his speech, there were mutterings of what could have been if he had been a prefect, maybe even the Head Boy. Our hearts were in favour, because he was respected and could sort out the indiscipline on campus quickly. Our heads disagreed, however, given that Baji had also gotten into trouble occasionally. Elevating him to a prefect role could, instead, have sent the wrong message to the student community. But that evening, everyone chose to dream. It was an emotional night. Although many juniors could not forget the past injustices they had received from this group of outgoing students, forgiveness was in the air.

The send-off was lavish. The choir performed a few songs, including some odd choices – our choirmaster's favourite was a requiem. By our school's standards, this event was a big deal. This was no ordinary send-off – the kitchen staff even served food. And the authorities chose to relax some of SAJOMACO's strictest rules that evening. Girls were permitted to hang around the dining hall well past the end of the event, something of an abomination normally, given the proximity to the boys' dormitories. And the party-like atmosphere continued well past midnight. No one policed the strict rule of separation of boys and girls that night. And it felt like no one believed that anyone would take advantage of the lax atmosphere. The students did not abuse the limited freedom they were given; instead, what permeated the atmosphere was a lot of heart-to-heart conversations, in one-on-one formats or huddles, with students doing their best to make the most of the limited time they had with each other. There were a lot of tears. It felt normal – and good. No other send-off party came close to this one during my time at SAJOMACO.

***

The most significant powershift for students happens in the second term, when the sixth-year students begin to focus on their final exams. For a small group of students whose behaviour would have caught the attention of the teachers in the previous years, the change is even more significant. These are the students who would be selected as prefects to run the affairs of the students. Often, half of the cohort of prefects would be the most academically able.

But being selected as a prefect also came with its own burdens and responsibilities, not the least of which was governance. In my fifth year, I was aware that I was part of this pool of candidates for my year. Of the many pros that came with being a prefect, the opportunity to bring some law and order back onto campus stood out the most. Reforms were long overdue, and, more importantly, I felt that if a group of students who were committed to improving the school were selected, they could reverse some of the rot that SAJOMACO was experiencing.

Usually, the selection of school prefects was a closed-door

affair amongst the teachers. After the Principal compiled the list of names – close to twenty, he made the announcement at the school assembly. As he read out the names, the assembly chatter went through the roof. Unsurprisingly, the top positions usually drew the most reaction from the crowd. Although predicting who was going to be made Head Boy or Head Girl was relatively easy, some announcements genuinely surprised everyone.

No fanfare accompanied the actual handover from the outgoing prefects to the incoming ones, and there were no inductions either. New prefects, having been thrown in at the deep end, were simply expected to get on with the job. The fact that they had spent a few years on campus, ideally observing past prefects, was enough in the eyes of the school authorities.

In January 1995, at the start of the second term of the 1994–95 academic year, the spotlight turned to my year for prefect selection. But this time around, the school decided to screen potential prefects by conducting panel interviews.

We were never told why the process took on this twist. Maybe it was because the teachers felt that the prefects in Wolex's year disappointed them, and that they should try something different for our year group. Some prefects in Wolex and Baji's year groups behaved just like some of the troublemakers in their respective years. Therefore, it made sense for the teachers to gauge the commitment of the students they were about to put into positions of authority, and see if they had any backbone too.

The panel of teachers conducting the interviews was mixed, about half a dozen or so. Some of the prefects in the retiring group put forward a recommendation or two as potential replacements for the teachers to consider. Nonetheless, the selection and ultimate decision rested with the panel.

It was a lazy afternoon. The sun was blazing hot; most of us were relaxing in the dormitory when a junior entered my room.

'Senior Bunmi, they said I should tell you to come to the chapel'.

He had raced down to deliver this message. He was panting as he blurted out the words.

'Who?' I asked.

'KwaKwa and the Chaplain and some teachers. I think they are trying to pick the new prefects'.

I made my way to the chapel, trying as best as possible to be calm. A few of my classmates were already there, waiting to be called in. My name rang out from deep within the chapel.

'Asaolu!'

'Good luck', someone mumbled, as I disappeared into the building.

After navigating my way through the pews, I came face to face with the panel.

'You understand why you are here, I'm sure', KwaKwa began. 'We are talking to some of you as we draw up a list of prefects for your year'.

'Yes, sir'.

'What position do you think we should put you in?'

'Assistant Head Boy, sir'.

Many had tipped me for the School Organist position, so my response raised a few eyebrows, for two reasons. First, I was good at playing the foot-pedal organ (I had won the prize for best music student in my first year). Second, I had been very active in the choir.

'That's interesting', Reverend Dahunsi, who was all too aware of my musical capabilities, said. 'Why AHB?'

Having worked closely with the Reverend for a few years, I knew his question was a loaded one. It also implied that he wanted to know why I didn't want to go for the position of Head Boy.

'I am quite sound, musically, but I think that I have much more to contribute as far as running the school's affairs is concerned. I will be underutilised if I am put in the Organist position. I think I'll do a good job as AHB'.

'But why not Head Boy?'

'Because I think Danksy is likely to become Head Boy. I am happy to support him as AHB'.

My frankness probably came as a bit of a surprise to the panel. But I knew that consensus was building around Danksy for the HB role. There was no point in creating a contest out of the process. What was more important was to have a strong and effective team that could run the school well. What Danksy lacked in height or stature, he made up for in charisma. Within the Christian clubs on campus, he had emerged as the most recognisable of the leaders, having been given the opportunity to express and develop his public speaking skills.

Apart from the panel interview, the prefect selection process departed from the norm in another way. Instead of filling all the positions immediately, despite the interviews, only eleven positions were filled when the first announcement was made. The rest came weeks later. It was as though the teachers wanted to be sure they got things right this time around. They even consulted with some of the eleven before making the second and final announcement.

Maintaining law and order with a full set of twenty or so

prefects was hard enough, talk less of eleven newbies. So, we were up against it from the very start. Thankfully, the most influential positions – Head Boy, Assistant Head Boy, Food, Labour and House Captains – were filled first. If this were a government, the equivalent would include the President, Vice President, Foreign Secretary, Minster of the Interior, and the like. Danksy was made Head Boy while I became Assistant Head Boy. Rex was given the Food Prefect portfolio while Bykes was selected as the Chapel Prefect.

In hindsight, the decision to appoint the first eleven was a blessing. The smaller group was easier to manage, and decision-making was not drawn out unnecessarily.

The new group established regular prefect meetings in which we deliberated on the major issues affecting the school. These meetings were frequent in the first few weeks after we resumed office, but reduced in frequency as law and order was re-established. We even took minutes. For fourteen-year-olds, this was novel. At the top of our priority list was the dining hall experience.

It was no coincidence that some of the brightest students ended up being prefects. Juggling the demands of normal student life with governance as a prefect was a challenging job. It was a sacrifice – and a thankless task, most of the time. Ironically, the more the teachers saw that we were effective, the more they backed away from their own supervisory duties. We ended up running pretty much all aspects of student life on campus, including but not limited to labour work. We had become reliable outsource agents for teachers.

Chapter 20

Within the first week after we became prefects, there were dramatic changes. And the speed caught us by surprise. The mundane ones included our moving from the floor of the dining hall to the top table, which was situated on a raised platform. An added benefit was that our food portions were more. But this was not news to us, having witnessed prefects in previous years. We were aware of some of these perks already.

What surprised us the most was that the students respected us more than we had expected. It didn't matter if an ant was the Head Boy; students respected the office – or at least they did at the very start, by default. This was decidedly new ground for us. Initially, we were worried that some of our classmates would make our lives difficult.

The dining hall was usually the first location where one could judge whether new prefects were going to be effective or not. Given that the dining hall experience had become disorderly before we became prefects, this was a big test for us. Asking students to form a queue had proved a waste of time, previously. But we had to function as prefects, so we asked them to form a queue. To our surprise, they did. Then we requested that they did not jump the queue. And they didn't.

I had longed to see the campus change over the years. Being the AHB, I was in a rare influential position to push through some of the ideas that I had been mulling over for years. The dining hall was priority, and the best place to test out these ideas.

Prefects in prior years had been uncoordinated in their approach to running the dining hall during mealtimes. Two or three prefects would walk the entire length of the hall within seconds of each other, barking out the same orders, leaving a gap behind for students who, wanting to steal or cause trouble, could get away with whatever they had in mind. The orders the prefects shouted out also worsened the cacophony and rowdiness in the hall.

Instead of each prefect conducting his own walkabout, independent of the other prefects, I suggested we divide the hall into segments, by groups of tables, and assign a prefect to each.

Each grid contained a maximum of six tables, or about sixty students. By being stationary, the prefect could see and monitor what was going on around him in real time. Unassigned prefects could provide additional assistance where required. So, whilst issues that occurred within a grid were primarily the responsibility of the grid prefect, he could call for assistance from prefects in adjacent segments or unassigned, roving prefects. This way, it was difficult for seniors who were bent on disrupting the order of the dining hall to carry out such plans.

We also decided that prefects should not eat until the students had finished their meals and left the hall. That way, we could concentrate on supervising proceedings.

The result was a complete turnaround in the dining hall

experience. Almost instantly, there was a halt to the bad habits that had characterised the experience: the rushing for food, the rowdiness and raucousness, the *cantabing*, the submission of more than one plate, and more. These changes took us back – or as close as possible – to my first-year days.

Emboldened by the initial positive response from the students, we moved quickly to other areas. Our next focus was the dormitories. We were determined to get the students to follow the school timetable, particularly for assembly and labour work. Students had no problem responding to the clanging of the bell when the chiming was a call to the dining hall. They greeted other bell notifications with a sluggish reaction. In the past, prefects and teachers were brutal in dealing with those students who dragged their feet, literally chasing them out with cudgels and whips. They flogged the students while they were bathing, even when, many times, the students ran late because of circumstances beyond their control, water scarcity being the most common reason. Even for a tough Nigerian kid, I always felt this was inhumane and indiscriminate.

Our group decided to be approachable, and that meant dispensing with the 'We are here to get you' attitude. We needed to win the hearts and minds of the juniors, not least because they could be helpful to us for intelligence gathering.

Instead of flushing students out of their dormitories by chasing them around with sticks and belts, I suggested that we simply stand outside the dormitories and initiate a countdown loud enough for everyone to hear.

'Akinyele House! We are giving you thirty seconds to wrap up whatever you are doing and exit the building!'

'Thirty...'

'Twenty-nine...'

'Twenty-eight...'

And so, the countdown carried on.

A thunderous rumble reverberated through the building, like a shock wave, fuelled by the brisk countdown, and a stream of students would begin pouring out onto the dormitory grounds. It was important for us to keep up appearances by looking as stern as possible. But it was difficult to keep a straight face when one noticed a ten-year-old whose attempt to dress in haste had left half of his face covered in talc powder or clothes hastily donned inside out. Some of the students noticed our softening exterior and grinned as they whizzed past us.

'Ten...'

'Nine...'

By now, everyone going past was smiling, mainly because they knew they were safe. One could still hear the rumbling of the stairs as the rest did their best to make it out on time.

'Five... four... three...'

Now the pressure was really on.

'Two...'

'One point nine...'

'One point eight...'

This was the real surprise that nobody was expecting. We wanted to introduce some grace to our countdown, but we were also conscious that appearances mattered. Too soft and the students would take advantage of us. We still looked like the prefects of old – sticks and belts in hand – but we had every intention of avoiding using these gadgets to chase anyone out. Once the countdown moved into decimals, the juniors started to laugh. It was a sight to behold, and a refreshing one too.

Accordingly, attendance and timeliness at assembly improved dramatically. The boys started to arrive at assembly before the girls.

During one of our meetings, I proposed to the team shortly before school broke up for holidays that, on our return, we bring with us powerful flashlights, and that we each return to campus a day earlier. That way, we would be better prepared to re-establish order on campus as students arrived. The flashlights were used to convey a sense of dread to any student who contemplated remaining in the dormitories during evening prep. We would walk up to a dormitory in darkness and abruptly, simultaneously, flick our lights on, and accompany the blitz with shouted instructions, warning any students of the consequences if we found them hiding in the rooms after the countdown was over.

The strategy worked.

On resumption day, we stationed ourselves at the gate, reassuring parents who might have had reasons to appeal to the school authorities about any issues affecting their children.

Reporting a case of bullying to a prefect, face to face, was more likely to lead to proper results than reporting it to staff. Once a prefect deemed a student's cause to be legitimate, the entire group of prefects took up the issue. Disrespecting one prefect meant disrespecting all. If one of our classmates was the cause of a junior's problems, we would collectively appeal to the senior in question on behalf of the student, because it was better to massage a senior's ego than confront it. If our classmate proved difficult, we would find other ways to protect the junior, and were happy to make a strong case against the senior to the school authorities.

The latter approach was rare, thankfully. And if said bully

was a year or two below us, he did not stand a chance.

The turnaround in the boys' dormitory was very visible to all. It was a different story for the girls, however. Although I suggested to the boys that we should reach out to them to offer our support or exchange ideas, we failed to reach a consensus. And because the boys had agreed to an all-or-nothing approach on major decisions, the suggestion did not stand a chance.

Some of the female prefects frustrated the laudable efforts of Fayz, the Head Girl. I felt sorry for her. Despite not having the full backing of the boys, I reached out at some point, letting her know that if she needed help, she should reach out.

An opportunity to collaborate did, eventually, come up, because of an incident that occurred in the boys' dormitory.

Chapter 21

Once we had stabilised the dining hall experience, and improved student response time to assembly and labour calls, we turned our attention to more challenging issues.

The cooking of 'raw' had become a scourge under previous regimes, a practice that had been allowed to get out of control. This was yet another slippery slope for us – a test that if we failed to decisively confront, could make life challenging for us afterwards.

It wasn't difficult to catch a student cooking raw. Most of the time it was rice being cooked, and the aroma made it easy to trace. That did not stop students trying their luck, however. In the first few months after we became prefects, the sixth-year students ahead of us continued to do as they pleased. We chose our battles carefully – there was no point aggravating a group of seniors who were on their way out. So, we ignored most of what they did – including the cooking of raw. For everyone else, however, we maintained a zero-tolerance approach.

Some of our classmates justified their cooking of raw by pointing out that food portions were the same size for everyone, regardless of age – that they were hungrier as a result. They had a valid argument, and it felt disingenuous of us prefects to criticise them because our food portions were bigger. But one of the reasons the school prohibited the cooking of raw was safety, and most students still complied with the rules.

To catch the rule-breakers, we regularly monitored and inspected the dormitories, a time-consuming effort. A more effective way was if students reported incidences to us. There were no hotlines or rewards for tip-offs. Yet, as the months went by, juniors chose to become informants willingly, because they felt they could trust us. These tip-offs were always accurate. Juniors had the option to report to the Akinyele House group prefects, of which I was a member, or to the group based around Okusanya House. Once a group was alerted to an incident, a runner would inform the other group, and, within minutes, we would descend on the room where the raw was being cooked.

Our school Principal, who was relatively new to the school after Ignominy had moved on, was emboldened by our success. He used our reinvigorated platform to draw up even tougher rules. He designated the cooking of raw and the stealing of mattresses as the worst two offences a student could commit. Anyone guilty of these offences would be suspended.

Initially, we reported raw cases to the school authorities. However, once the penalty of suspension was implemented, the prefects unanimously decided to stop reporting, because we felt the consequences for the students were severe. Instead, we decided to seize and destroy the raw ourselves. We had grown so much in confidence that we could call even our classmates to order. However, while we simply discarded their raw or turned it into compost, we punished any guilty junior. Gradually, students' behaviour changed, and they didn't need a prefect to force them to do the right thing. Even better, some students joined in the 'policing' of the campus. This was most evident in the first term of our final year when a few of the prefects with the most significant portfolios, including myself, did not resume on campus with the rest of the students, in order to sit our final exams early, away from school. We would still sit a second (proper) one at SAJOMACO a few months later. Although our teachers frowned at our decision, they could not stop us.

Our absence from school left a vacuum, depleting the core group of the prefect cohort. After the exams, I returned for a couple of weeks before term ended, and stood in for Danksy as Head Boy. Danksy, Rex and a few others stayed back at home instead. I met a fully functioning school, as some of our closest friends, like Jetta and Koko, who were not prefects, had stepped in to support the remaining prefects. It was satisfying to hear that the student body had embraced the makeshift arrangement. And this had happened without any official announcement.

A few days after I returned, one evening a runner brought a message to me in Akinyele House that some students were up to no good in one of the extension dormitories. Under the cover of darkness, I gathered as many prefects as I could and we descended on the area, surrounding it completely. I stormed into the dimly lit dormitory with Niyeh, the Okusanya House prefect. What confronted us almost made our jaws drop. There, in front of us, were two fourth-year students, two years our junior. But not just any random fourth-year students. These were girls! In the boys' dormitory!

There are shocking events that happened on campus which become legendary, years later. But *this*? This was the equivalent of seeing a black swan. It just didn't happen. What was even more infuriating was that it had happened under our watch, after all the steps we had taken to encourage students to abide by the school rules.

'What in the world…', I began.

Two of our classmates had facilitated the girls' entry into the dormitory, deciding to gamble on the relaxed mood which permeated the campus because exams were over. Given the seriousness of the situation, they leapt to make a case for clemency.

'AHB, cool temper. It's our fault. Don't take it out on them', Demu said. Peer pressure had turned him into a bit of a troublemaker. However, I was still surprised that he would get involved in something like this.

'What kind of rubbish is this? You guys are in serious *wahala*! Girls in the boys' dormitory? *E ti da'ran o*[6]? What do you think the Principal will say *na*?' I shook my head. I still couldn't believe my eyes.

'Asha, c'mon now. I'm sure we can work something out'. Asha was a shortened form of my surname.

'Work out *kini*?' I demanded. 'My friend, you're in trouble', I said dismissively, as I pushed past him.

I levelled the coldest stare I could muster as I approached the girls. Committing a serious offence in the girls' dormitory was bad enough. But this was in the boys' dormitory. Our turf. We had to make these girls fully grasp the gravity of the situation they were in – to send the mother of all chills down their spine.

Niyeh started the interrogation.

---

[6] You are in trouble.

'Tell me, how did you two process in your medulla oblongata that it was right to come into a boys' dormitory?' His question was met with silence. He paused for a few more seconds, hoping for a response. None came. 'Are you two deaf? You clearly don't get it. I'm going to make your lives hell if you don't start talking and give me some answers!'

The girls' body language exuded disdain rather than fear. These were two of the unruliest girls in their year group; a lack of respect for authority was in their DNA, so their attitude was not surprising. But we were the authority figures in this situation, and we were going to make that abundantly clear.

'Get up right now! You are both deluded, thinking this will go away somehow, or because you have some sugar daddy-wannabe looking at you, who you think will save you both. You're mistaken', Niyeh said.

Reluctantly, they got up, but one kissed her teeth in the process.

Wham!

Niyeh landed a slap on her left cheek. Culturally, Niyeh's action would not have shocked anyone. And even though our prefect group didn't punish students as much as our predecessors, we still slapped and flogged students, just like other seniors. It was part of the culture we had inherited. But the slap came as a surprise to her.

'Have you lost your mind?' he ordered. 'You better wake up!'

Demu rushed to shield the girls from additional slaps. This time his tone was pleading. The girl who had been slapped started to sob, her normal stone-cold demeanour dissolving in tears.

Demu and his partner in crime begged us to find a private

place to discuss how they might navigate their way out of the situation.

The default response to such a flagrant incident would be to march the girls straight to the Principal's house. Their actions guaranteed them a suspension, at best; at worst, expulsion. Either way, the consequences would be dire. Everyone knew it. The stakes were very high indeed. Demu and his friend were also likely to be punished.

So began the pleading and negotiations for the next ten minutes on the side balcony of the dormitory, with many students looking on from afar. The surroundings resembled a crime scene, as the other prefects had cordoned off the area.

Niyeh and I took some space to consider our decision. For all his showboating, Niyeh was a nice chap. But he had one final move to make. He wanted to milk the situation even more, for effect. Rarely were we presented with the opportunity to catch students breaking a serious rule red-handed like this. Niyeh asked me to indulge a little further in some play acting.

'Never! We can't allow it!' he shouted in my face, so that others could hear.

'Well...'. I pretended to consider his words, like I was taking him seriously, while trying my best to keep my composure.

'What kind of nonsense...?' He stormed back into the dormitory and started threatening to take the girls straight to the Principal's house.

The two boys pleaded with me, as the highest-ranking prefect on campus, to calm Niyeh down.

'Guys', I began, 'I can try, but I can't argue with Niyeh. What do you expect us to do? And this is not my jurisdiction. Niyeh is the prefect in charge of this since Okusanya House where he stays is closer than my Akinyele House. So, if he says we must report this incident to the Principal, I can't stand in his way'.

My response, though designed to serve the deception, was in fact a serious point of consideration, based on a silent code the prefects had adopted: if just one prefect disagreed with the others regarding an infraction, the incident had to be reported.

We let the crazy show carry on for a few more minutes. It had to be that way to erase the arrogance the girls had displayed when first confronted. A few minutes later, we told them we had grudgingly agreed to make an exception in this case and find a way not to escalate the incident to the school authorities.

'Thank you! God will reward your kindness'.

Dismissing their response, we explained that it was one thing not to report the incident, but another thing entirely to escape punishment. The latter was not going to happen.

With the immediate issue settled, our attention shifted to the next major headache confronting us – the safe return of the girls to their dormitory. This was a risky venture, because it had to be done covertly, and the boys' dormitory locked down to allow their safe passage. The bigger challenge was to get the girls to the other side of the campus, somehow evading Bentigor, the maniacal security guard, and his gun.

We not only had to enable the girls to escape but we had to accompany them, and provide the cover they needed. It took about ten minutes to escort them successfully to a safe zone in the girls' dormitory area, right under Bentigor's nose.

The other prefects and I returned to Akinyele House after-wards, for a debrief. We still couldn't believe what we had just witnessed, but there was work to do.

During the debrief, we learned that while Niyeh and I had been completely focused on the incident involving the girls, the rest of the prefects had confiscated two raws in the area. The prefects involved had also decided not to report these to the school authorities, and, instead, simply destroyed the food. Punishment would be meted out later in the morning, but it was important to prevent the complete derailment of the students' academic prospects. Notwithstanding, given the seriousness of the events of that evening, part of us wished we had made a scapegoat out of one of those students. We wondered whether we had been too gracious.

Once the girls returned to their dormitory, as far as punishing them directly was concerned we were powerless. We had to rely instead on influencing our female counterparts. The next morning, I told Fayz, the Head Girl, what had transpired and asked her to ensure she picked things up from where we had left them. Unfortunately, the punishment the girls received was nowhere close to what we felt matched the seriousness of their offence. This was clearly a case of 'the two that got away', and the relatively lenient punishment they got did not help the delicate balance we were striking to achieve in addressing offences.

***

Term soon ended and we all left for the Christmas holidays. When we returned in January, the full team of prefects was back in action. Some teachers continued to grumble about the decision of some prefects not to return to school the previous term. In the end, we got on with our lives.

Life carried on as normal, but the prefects who were absent

during the final two weeks of the previous term requested that we provide them with a rundown of what had transpired. After interrogating Niyeh and me, they criticised our decision not to have reported the students to the authorities. Our reasoning fell on deaf ears. They argued that the seriousness of the matter warranted a show of force.

'At the expense of the future of these girls?' I asked.

'You guys were too soft on them *jare*. This was a red line that should never have been crossed. These girls should have been punished'.

I was stunned that my colleagues, who at the time were hundreds of kilometres away, were quick to rush to judgement. No amount of explanation to provide some context swayed them. So, I gave up. Maybe a better opportunity would present itself.

A few days later, a runner came to find me in my room. The Okusanya House group of prefects needed me to attend to an urgent issue.

There were four other prefects there, including Danksy. My presence was required because, as the second-most senior prefect, they needed my consent on a major decision they were about to make.

Also in the room was a junior in the year below us. He was the archetype of those students we had avoided in previous years, because they were extremely rude. Their attitude mostly changed once we became prefects, although one or two still tried to defy us on the rare occasion. A student who let his emotions get the better of him and disrespected a prefect would become the most wanted person on campus. A fourth-year student did just that during our tenure. We dispatched a squad to apprehend him and deliver him to Akinyele House where a council of prefects was meeting. Each prefect took his turn to flog him.

Our classmate, Jelo, heard the commotion and burst into the room to investigate. Unfortunately for the junior, he had offended Jelo in the past.

'Oh, it's this one. I didn't realise'. Turning to the prefects, he added, 'Please, carry on teaching him a lesson *jare*', before turning his back and leaving.

Returning to the evening in question, one of the prefects tried to bring me up to speed.

'Asha, so, Derin did something wrong this evening. He has apologised for his actions. We just wanted you to know'.

'Sorry, I'm not sure I understand. What did he do?'

'Well, basically, he stole a mattress. The junior who owns the mattress reported the theft, so we investigated and confirmed. We've punished Derin though'.

'So, what are you asking me to do here?' I asked, ignoring the terrified Derin.

'You know that the Principal has made stealing mattresses a serious offence, one that will automatically lead to Derin's expulsion if he finds out. We just wanted to make sure we are all on the same page here'.

'Absolutely, we are all on the same page', I assured him. 'I'm ready'.

I turned to Derin and said, 'You're ready to head over to the Principal's house now, *abi*?'

Immediately, everybody started to talk over each other.

'Bunmi, now, we need to think of Derin's future here. Show some mercy'.

'Mercy *ko*, mercy *ni*'. I replied, keeping my voice even. '*Shey* you considered mercy when Niyeh and I explained to you

205

about the incident of last term, with the girls in the boys' dormitory'.

I turned to Derin. This was my opportunity to carve deeply into a wound and rub in as much salt as possible. I fully intended to make the most of it.

'*Bros*, it's not my fault', I said to him, shrugging. 'I am simply abiding by an agreement we prefects have to offences like yours'. With that, I strode over to the door of the room and walked out in the direction of the Principal's house.

Derin ran after me, as did some of the Okusanya House-based prefects, pleading with me to reconsider. I walked a further hundred metres before I halted and gave the entire group a telling off, accusing them of being hypocritical.

I had no intention of following through on my threat to report Derin, but I needed to drum home the message that we were not robots, and must use our discretion when the stakes were high enough to negatively impact the future of the student in question.

Such events caused tensions within our prefect group, exposing us to the fact that governance is not entirely black and white; that the grey may be dominant. Cracks appeared from time to time, testing the unity of our group, and exposing our differences. We learned that compromise was not a sign of weakness, but a necessary ingredient if a team were to succeed. And, ultimately, we were responsible for the well-being of people first; the rules that governed them should always be a means to an end, not the end itself.

Chapter 22

Time flies when one is having fun. The opposite is true also. The first few years at SAJOMACO seemed to drag on forever, and it felt like the senior years would never arrive, talk less of imagining the final year, month, or day at boarding school. But final year did arrive, eventually, and it is one that most of us look back to with a sense of nostalgia. In my case, the flashbacks are accompanied with many what-ifs.

As prefects, we ended up being victims of our own success, in a way. By effectively restoring the school to order, we had freed up the teachers. Gone were the days when they were highly visible, maintaining discipline on the school grounds. As such, one would think we had built enough goodwill with the teachers that they would be understanding when we needed them to be.

We were wrong.

The swearing-in ceremony for the prefects happened towards the end of their tenure, not the beginning. For my year group, the ceremony went ahead, shortly after the incident with the girls in the boys' dormitory, just before Christmas of 1995, complete with all the pomp and glamour that such an occasion demands. Official photographs with the Principal and other members of staff were taken afterwards. Prefects like Danksy and Rex, who did not return to school after taking their external final exams, were effectively erased from the official photographic records. I felt that the decision by the school authorities to hold the ceremony, despite knowing that the other prefects – especially Danksy – were absent was harsh, but I was powerless to do anything about it.

After school resumed in January 1996, we did not dwell much on the school's decision about the swearing-in ceremony. Focus shifted back to running the school and preparing for our (second) final exams. But, given that these exams were going to be similar to the ones some of us had sat a few months prior, classes became less interesting. We had already covered most of the material being taught. We tried to balance the boredom setting in with respecting our teachers and fellow students.

We were flying high. Soon, the school would announce a new group of prefects for the year below us and we would gain even more freedom. Some of us were consulted to suggest suitable replacement candidates.

It was customary for the school to hold a valedictory service to celebrate and send off the final-year students, and so preliminary plans were being drawn up. Meanwhile, various houses were also discussing plans for their own send-off events. The events were shaping up to be the most spectacular the school had seen in decades.

We had a few weeks left before handing over the reins. One of the most challenging aspects of our remit was carrying our classmates along whilst keeping the difficult ones in check. An overbearing regime invariably may lead to confrontation, perhaps even a head-on collision. This was a constant threat. However, the fact that we were not complete strangers to our classmates helped. In fact, some of the most difficult students were friends with a few prefects – and their friendships pre-dated SAJOMACO. So, when a group of boys marched on Okusanya House to rough up a prefect, the presence of a prefect-ally like Jetta neutralised their angst. In contrast, too lax a governance culture may result in one's own classmates taking full advantage. Both a heavy-handed approach and a relaxed style result in the undermining – or worse, a complete loss – of authority.

While it was clear that we had restored order on campus, some of our classmates preferred how life used to be. Although the school authorities took their time to carefully select the prefects, they ended up with a narrow group: most of the prefects happened to be leaders of a Christian drama group. To some of our classmates, it was as though this group had hijacked the governance of student affairs or that the school bestowed too much power on us. It is true that the prefect group could have been more diverse. Certainly, there were other students who could have made the group more balanced. But it was difficult to blame the school authorities, given that their intentions appeared to be honourable. As for the prefects, we simply encouraged the students to follow the rules. We made mistakes too, however. Occasionally, some prefects behaved like they were on a power trip. Notwithstanding, both the teachers and students could observe that the school had turned a corner. We managed, as best as we could, our dissenting classmates, through diplomacy, and by showing them respect, whilst being firm where necessary. We realised early on that it was easier to achieve our aims if the cohort of prefects worked together as a group. Breaking ranks or going on a solo mission was just not wise. Despite our best efforts, however, the tension persisted.

As we began counting down the days towards the handover, life for us was as close as it could get to running on autopilot. A full team of prefects was no longer required to maintain order in the dining hall. The students knew full well that we followed through on our threats if someone broke the rules.

Little did we know that a major test lay around the corner, one which would have major implications for our year group, as well as the entire school.

***

It was a calm, but sunny afternoon. The Principal had a job for us. Compared with his predecessors, like Ignominy, he was a breath of fresh air initially. We grew fond of him. However, as the months went by, his halo dimmed because of the way he started to relate to us. He cancelled the interhouse sports competition and halted the popular social night event. For the prefects, it was as if we had become an expedition force, or a group of mercenaries, who he could call upon to execute missions for him. And the more he exercised his authority as Principal by asking us to fix a problem, the more it underscored our feeling that we were no longer partners in solving governance issues on campus. We were simply soldiers who were there to execute his orders.

The task the Principal wanted us to carry out required him to come down from his residence, near the chapel, all the way to the boys' dormitory to deliver the message personally. What was notable about this task, though, was that he felt the need to summon as many prefects as he could. This struck me as a little odd, arguably over the top.

'Why did it take ten minutes to find you people?'

He was clearly angry because some of the prefects had been away from their dormitories at a drama rehearsal. Some prefects were still missing, but he seemed content with the number that had assembled.

'I have an important assignment for you, one you cannot afford to bungle'.

'Yes, sir'.

'I need you to go and find one of your classmates. I think they call him Rooz. Bring him to my house. He has been suspended, but I am told that he has disregarded the suspension and has come back onto the school grounds. And he's wearing uniform to blend in. Can you imagine? That idiot of a boy. Somebody told me that he has been stealing mattresses and taking them to town to sell them. I just finished speaking to a boy's father who was very angry because he claimed that someone stole his son's mattress. I won't be surprised if it was this same Rooz that stole it. And you people are on campus while this has been happening?'

None of us responded.

'I made it clear that anybody who steals a mattress on this campus will get suspended. Automatic suspension. *Abi* you don't understand? How come you people haven't caught anybody recently? Or are you going to use your upcoming exams as an excuse? Ah, I see. Maybe you are already thinking of handing over to the next set. I have news for you. You still have work to do'.

Still none of us said a word.

'Rooz must be apprehended and brought straight to me. Do you hear me?'

'Yes, sir'.

This task should have been straightforward, in theory. In practice, however, it was the kind of request that ignored the fact that diplomacy had helped us thus far. Rooz was our classmate, not a junior, and he had several friends who were in the bad books of the school. Given that our tenure was almost over, we had become less aggressive in chasing down relatively minor infractions committed by our classmates, feeling there was little to be gained from such cavalier moves. That made this otherwise supposedly straightforward request a tinder keg. Yet, refusing to carry it out was not an option. If not handled well, we potentially faced a lose–lose situation.

Most of the students observing us did not think much of the presence of the Principal and the prefects surrounding him. This sort of briefing, where staff would visit and interact with prefects, had become normal again. However, his facial and hand gestures would certainly have indicated his message was serious.

Once the Principal had given us his instructions, he returned to his house. We headed straight to the dormitory area where we believed Rooz was likely to be lodging. Our movement raised some eyebrows because it was unusual to see a delegation of prefects approaching a building without cause, and there was no raw being cooked. As much as we tried to disperse our group, there was a good chance that we might need all hands on deck to forcibly seize Rooz and escort him to the Principal.

He was nowhere to be found around the dormitories, but a credible lead was provided that he could be found hanging out with some students – boys and girls – in one of the classrooms. Even without a lead, we probably would have sent a runner ahead to check out this location. The school forbade students getting involved in relationships, but could not legislate against platonic friendships, or students having conversations in the open.

About ten of us approached and swiftly surrounded the sixth-year classroom block where Rooz was. Danksy and bulky Samba went in first to explain to Rooz that the Principal had demanded that he leave the school grounds, but only after coming to see him at his house. A small commotion arose as the students he was with tried to create a scene. It was too good an opportunity for them to ignore. Somehow, however, we managed to keep the situation under control, thanks largely to Rooz's cooperation.

He told us that he'd like to head over to the dormitory, and then to Mr Fado's house, our music teacher, before heading to the Principal's house. He wanted to change into mufti from the uniform he was wearing. That way, he wouldn't antagonise the Principal when he saw him. We obliged.

Mr Fado was Rooz's guardian. Sometimes, students who were suspended simply didn't have anywhere to go if they had no relatives in Owo town. So, if a master was prepared to lodge them temporarily, they jumped at the opportunity. Mr Fado had been very protective of Rooz since he joined the school in our fourth year. Once, when a senior bullied Rooz, Mr Fado came looking for the senior and beat him up until he fainted. Some masters were not to be messed around with.

As we walked Rooz back from the classroom area to the boys' dormitory, word was spreading about our mission. Seeing a group of prefects escorting someone like Rooz was far from a normal occurrence. Any hopes we had that we could carry out this mission discreetly were misplaced. Nonetheless, we had the situation under control.

Things took a turn as we approached Okusanya House. We had just reached a small triangular patch of field tucked in between it, an incinerator, and the library when, out of nowhere, Bentigor burst onto the scene, a hunter's rifle grasped in one hand.

'Hey, hey, hey, what is he doing here?' one of Rooz's friends shouted, pointing at a fast approaching Bentigor.

'Na im wey dem suspend, *abi?*' Bentigor barked at Rooz, ignoring Rooz's friend.

'*Abeg*, don't pour kerosene on fire, *Oga* Bentigor', a prefect begged. 'We have this under control'. Rooz, now visibly agitated, grew angry.

'Rooz, please ignore this man. We are not working with him', another added.

A view that one of Rooz's friends had floated when we had first found him, that the Principal and the prefects had colluded to nab him, may have been playing on his mind, and Bentigor's appearance made it seem as if the entire school apparatus had been set in motion with the sole intent to trap him.

'*Ehn ehn*, you come carry me with *shakabula abi*? *Sebi* I be bahd guy for school. Come dey carry me den', he said tauntingly to Bentigor.

'I go shoot am *o!*' Bentigor warned.

'Who sent this madman here, for God's sake? *Oga* Bentigor, *abeg*, can you just *disfarahan*[7]?' Samba told him. 'Who sent you anyway?'

'*Oga* Principal said I must bring am, now'.

'Tell *Oga* Principal he is coming with us. *Abeg, commot*'.

---

[7]   Disappear.

We eventually managed to convince Bentigor to leave, but by this time, every eye was transfixed on the unfolding drama. We escorted Rooz to his dormitory, then on to Mr Fado's house, back through the dormitory area, down the main artery of the school to the staff office, and, finally, to the Principal's house. Rooz hadn't changed his clothes.

The Principal's house was rather majestic, a throwback to colonial times. Compared with the other staff residences on campus, it was palatial, the only residential building on campus for staff that was not a bungalow. Few students ever stepped inside the hallowed halls of the reception area, let alone the rest of the house. The power accorded to the Principal was almost dictatorial.

The house was situated at the intersection of three roads on the school grounds. One led to the girls' dining hall, the second to the staff office, and the third to the chapel, before continuing on to the boys' dormitory area. Directly in front of the house towered a large mango tree, with a monster-sized earth bed supporting it. On the rare occasion when the atmosphere was relaxed, students could be found under the tree, taking cover from the unrelenting heat of the sun.

When we arrived, we found the Principal seated on a raffia cane chair on the porch. The atmosphere was tense. It was an uneven match. There we were, at least ten prefects, man-marking just one student in the form of a semicircle.

'So, you are Rooz?' the Principal began.

'Yes, sir', he replied, his voice quiet.

'Get down on your knees!'

It was important to the Principal that he put Rooz in his place. Having a conversation with the two of them standing would be perceived as the height of disrespect.

215

'What part of the word "suspension" don't you understand? You have the audacity to be wearing this uniform when you have been suspended'.

Rooz avoided eye contact, and stared into the distance.

'Answer me, you good-for-nothing fool! I do not want to see your shadow anywhere near these grounds. Do you understand?'

For rebellious students like Rooz, this exchange with the Principal could tarnish his reputation. He had to show some defiance, especially with the prefects watching.

'But I don't know what I did to get a suspension, sir. It's not fair', he began.

The Principal stared at him.

'Did I hear you correctly? You—' Rooz cut him off mid-sentence.

'I didn't do anything wrong'.

'You are a bastard', the Principal spat. 'In this school, you and others like you have no place. I'll deal with every single one of you'.

Rooz couldn't resist.

'There's nothing you can do', he taunted.

'Your time here is up', the Principal roared. He made his way down the stairs.

Whoosh!

The slap took Rooz by surprise, who no doubt had expected to be flogged, but that would require a cane, which the Principal did not have in his hand. We were also surprised. This was a little out of character for the Principal. But the way Rooz had spoken to him must have infuriated him, especially with the rest of us watching.

Rooz shrieked and collapsed to the ground.

'My eyes! Yeee! How dare you?' He was half-crying, half-shouting.

Wham!

He was cut short with another ringing slap. The prefects looked at each other, uneasily. We had a rapidly deteriorating situation on our hands. The Principal dealt several more blows to Rooz's face, whilst holding onto him to prevent his escape.

The typical response of any student caught in a situation like this would be to cut his or her losses and run. Physically striking the Principal was not an option, as that would guarantee expulsion. At one point, Rooz appeared to have tried to strike the Principal. Samba quickly stepped in and discouraged him from doing so. If Rooz had hit the Principal, when the dust settled and blame apportioned, culture would most certainly support the Principal, the authority figure.

Recognising that Rooz had now become a flight risk, the Principal gripped his collar to prevent him escaping and continued to rain slaps down on him.

Rooz struggled, but the Principal would not let go. When he managed to wriggle out of his shirt, the Principal grabbed his belt.

'Strip him naked!' he ordered us.

We could not believe what we were hearing, but we had no time to process it properly.

'I said, strip him naked! Did you hear me?' he barked.

It was the beginning of the end, what would turn out to be the most embarrassing, shameful episode of my time spent at SAJOMACO. It was one thing to be on the right side of law and order; it was a completely different thing to demean another student in such a manner.

We hesitated, limiting our involvement to holding Rooz so

that he wouldn't escape. Once the Principal realised that we weren't doing enough to get Rooz's clothes off him, he asked one of the security men to join him.

'Francis. See how rude this boy is?' The Principal started making his case to the security man who by then had responded to his request to help remove Rooz's clothes.

When elderly Yoruba people want to escalate a situation in which a younger person has disrespected them, they might claim that the younger person wants to assault them.

'He wants to beat me *o*. Can you imagine?'

By now, Rooz was half naked. If only we had made a stand, said something or pleaded on his behalf, but our individuality and sense of moral solidarity was lost in a tidal wave of authoritarian pressure.

The deed was done in less than a minute. The poor chap curled up in shame, protecting whatever he could of his dignity. But that was not the end of Rooz's misery. The Principal instructed Francis to tie Rooz's hands and feet up, separately, to complete his humiliation. This was the kind of treatment reserved for a common thief in town.

Our inability to consult each other to reach a consensus continued to cripple us. The Principal carried on lecturing, jubilant over his conquest of this once-stubborn, now crushed soul. Our faces were drained of life as we struggled to reconcile what we had just witnessed, what we had just been a part of.

Rooz was no Jesus, but a Judas feeling had descended upon us. If we could right this wrong episode, or rewrite it completely, we would do so without hesitation. There were other options the Principal could have chosen. He could have called one or two security guards and got them to escort Rooz out of the campus. Or hand him over to the police, given the allegation of theft. The decision to strip him naked was already a step too far, but tying him up like an animal was just too much to comprehend. If only we knew what lay ahead.

The girls' dining hall was just a stone's throw away from the Principal's house, and some of the girls had witnessed the episode from there, having gathered, waiting for the bell to ring. Despite the distance, they worked out what was going on. Within a few minutes, Rooz's younger sister had been informed and made a dash for the Principal's house, accompanied by some of her friends. She was wailing hysterically as she approached the house.

She didn't deliberate over what item of clothing to bring her brother. She rushed forward with what appeared to be a long scarf, or a bedsheet, and did her best to restore some dignity to him.

As far as the Principal was concerned, the episode was over. He had made it clear to Rooz, to us, and to whomever may have been watching who the boss was.

But he miscalculated. His actions were about to kick-start a demonstration the school had never seen the likes of before.

Chapter 23

After lecturing us for a few more minutes, the Principal dismissed the prefects. The sun had started to set when I reached Akinyele House. A few of our classmates were relaxing on the grand stairs behind Akinyele House as was their custom, waiting for the dining hall bell to ring. Opposite them was a science laboratory where girls who wanted to see their boyfriends covertly would hang out. The boys were mulling over some of the developments they had witnessed earlier when the prefects were escorting Rooz.

'Na real wa for this Principal *sha*', Omoh began. 'Make im com scatta everytin *patapata*[8]'.

'Don't mind the bastard. Can you imagine? Who cancels interhouse sports?' another chipped in.

'Or social night'.

'Double standards. I hear he don come entertain babes for im house'.

'Wetin?'

'Wetin what? You no see girls trooping in and out of dia. Yet, him come dey ration our gari by banning everytin'.

---

[8]   Completely.

'He de craze? I go show am I be *were*[9] one day. *Shey* you hear me'.

'Omoh, dem say the Principal wanted to see Rooz because he was suspended, just like you'.

'*Sebi* I finish my suspension now?' Omoh replied. 'For something wey I no fit do. Dem say I beat up dat babe because my name be similar, when *walai* I be for hostel'.

'Chai, you get bad luck *o*'.

'Wait now. I told them, but you know dem staff have ears only for what dem wan hear. What's that master's name again? Fatu. He just said I was the one. Gave me letter, say make I pack my bags and go on suspension'.

'But Rooz sef be careless *sha*, walking for campus like say he no know Principal eye de go to and fro. I no feel sorry for am *jare*'.

'Is this Rooz's sister?' Jelo pointed towards the science building.

'Yes, but I see another five girls with her. I think they are crying *o*'.

The boys got up and went to meet them. Once Rooz's sister explained what had happened, all hell broke loose. The boys led the girls back to the Principal's house. Seeing Rooz on the floor tied up enraged them even more.

'*Ko ni da fun e!*[10]'

The students cursed the Principal as they threw stones indiscriminately at the building. They also damaged an abandoned bus that was parked to the side of the house. The Principal barricaded himself inside while the students

---

9   Mad person.

10   A curse translating loosely as 'It won't be better for you'.

221

continued to rain down missiles on the building. Eventually, Rooz was set free by the boys and joined them in the attack.

Back in the dormitories, one could feel the tension in the air. As darkness descended, students who felt aggrieved by what had happened to Rooz grew louder in expressing their anger. Random shouts echoed through the halls.

'You won't get away with this! We no go 'gree *o*, we no go 'gree'.

I huddled with some students, both prefects and non-prefects, in a room on the first floor in Akinyele House.

Sage walked in on us. 'What's going on guys? It's like someone flipped a switch somewhere. Boys are mad *o*'.

'You didn't hear? In fact, where have you been sef?'

Sage was one of the prefects who was missing when the Principal asked us to look for Rooz. So, he was clueless as to what had happened.

'Guy, you don't know? Principal came and told these guys to go and fetch Rooz because he was on suspension and was still on campus', Jetta began.

'*Ehn*, so?'

'The man stripped the boy naked and tied him up like a goat'.

'Wat!'

'Yes *o*'.

'But you guys know that this is not the first time a teacher will strip someone naked', Sage said.

'No *o*. I'm not aware of that', Koko said.

'It was KwaKwa now. You guys didn't know? We were in the third year, I think. I was outside my room, on the steps, you know those back rooms. That's how KwaKwa was driving past in his 504. He saw me, slowed down to a stop and shouted at me that I should come to him. What was my offence? I was shirtless. I had my shorts on *o*. I don't know when not wearing a shirt became a crime in this *ogba*[11].

'Chai. Wickedness', Jetta interrupted.

'So, that's how this man decided to take off my shorts, leaving me with only my underwear. Madness'.

'You didn't run?'

'I didn't even think about running because I didn't know he was going to do that. Anyway, everybody in the dorm could see what was happening from their windows, even as far as Okusanya.

'Did anybody come to rescue you?'

'Not exactly, but come and see curses *ehn*. Even seniors that had bullied me before were shouting. Nobody was afraid'.

'That KwaKwa, *ehn*, may God deal with him'.

'Clearly, it's not just KwaKwa that can strip people naked. But Principal has two heads *sha*. Tying people up. He no even fear'.

'*Abi o*. Anyway, you people need to leave this place', Jetta said. 'You are now marked people'.

'Is it that serious?' Samba asked, defensively. 'It's understandable how people are feeling, but it was the Principal's fault, ultimately, not ours'.

'Are you sure you want to find out whether they will differentiate between him and you? I really think you should all find somewhere to escape to. Have you forgotten that a few years ago the Head Boy at Idoani in this same Ondo State was killed?'

'I agree with Jetta', Koko added. 'This situation could easily, rapidly, spin out of control'.

---

[11] Campus.

'This is crazy now'.

'Crazy is them finding you here and beating you up, in retaliation. It's time to *vamoos*'.

I looked around the room. Jetta and Koko were right, as we would soon find out. The situation was spiralling out of control. Gangs of students who had felt hard done by over the period we had been serving as prefects were plotting to use the Rooz incident as cause for exacting revenge.

There was no time to consult with the Okusanya prefects. We could only hope they were having a similar conversation and would reach the same conclusion. It was time to take cover. Every boy for himself. Dinner had just been served, but it would have been a suicide mission for any prefect to enter the dining hall and attempt to conduct proceedings, as if it were any normal day.

I left Akinyele House through the rear, along with Bykes, hoping to find somewhere safe enough to hide, and something to eat. Samba and Sage stayed behind, along with the other non-prefects. Samba usually could defend himself and Sage wasn't part of the group of prefects that took Rooz to the Principal's house. That was the logic. The staff quarters next to the boys' dormitory area was too risky, so we decided to head in the opposite direction, towards the girls' dormitory area. The Chaplain's house was amongst those furthest away from the boys' dormitory area. The other option was the Principal's house. At least we knew he was home, and if anyone could appreciate the gravity of the situation we were in, and the obligation the school had to provide us refuge, surely it had to be him.

The Principal admitted us, and his house became our base camp from which, powerless, we watched the school descend into chaos.

There was no way to communicate with the Okusanya prefects, and having effectively abandoned our post, we could only wonder how the normal functioning of the school day – what was left of it – would run.

By now, we would have asked for the bell to be rung to alert the hungry students to head over to the hall. Instead, angry shouts continued to ring out from the dormitories. A hungry man is an angry man, and the mob was already incensed and vengeful. The students descended on the dining hall as they did back when life was chaotic, and lawlessness reigned. Doors were kicked down. Food was stolen. Plates were smashed.

As Jetta had presciently warned, the angry mob surged, intent on its rampage, hellbent on finding prefects and destroying school property. Some of us had siblings in junior years. They were now targets too. As the melee unfolded, I left my brother Yemsta in the custody of the wise Jetta, Sage and Koko, hoping and praying that he would remain safe.

I would later find out that Yemsta had been forced to flee the dormitory too, making his escape with Sage and Topsy, Bykes' brother. Some students had spotted Sage on the balcony, and raced upstairs to beat him up. Luckily for him, Bros Abi, a classmate who was at least five years older than us, was near. He probably started school much later than us. He defended Sage from the mob and declared that he wasn't to be harmed. Samba too almost got beaten up. One of our classmates had chased him around the building, hoe in hand.

Sage realised it wasn't safe to hang around. To blend in and escape undetected, he dressed to match the rampaging students they were trying to evade: loose t-shirts, housewear shirts tied around their waists, and bandanas. They ran unchallenged through the main artery of the school road network, past the girls' dormitory area, till they reached Mr Fatu's house.

On seeing them, he opened the door and pointed a gun at them.

'Who are you? If you come one step closer, I'll fire!'

'It's me, sir. Sage. Don't shoot. The boys are rioting and looking for the prefects'.

'What happened?'

'The Principal stripped Rooz naked and tied him up. When the boys heard, they were angry'.

'*Ehn ehn*, isn't that the boy that was suspended?'

'Yes, sir'.

'What are those boys I see in the distance doing? Are they looking for you?'

Some of the boys had figured out Sage's steps and tracked him down.

'Yes, they must have seen us leave the boys' dormitory area'.

Without warning, Mr Fatu pointed his gun in the air and pulled the trigger.

Bang! Bang!

The approaching group dispersed immediately.

What had started as a demonstration in pockets of the student community eventually turned into a full-blown riot. Destruction of school property intensified. Both dining halls were attacked. Staff members were not safe. The school was no longer governable. Because this had moved into civil disobedience territory, the Principal went for the nuclear option: anti-riot police.

A request for the anti-riot police should not be undertaken lightly, because their presence can exacerbate an already fraught situation. In Nigeria speak, they only hear 'go', not 'come'. A civilian, like our Principal, could do no more than look on and hope for the best, once the anti-riot squad arrived. It would be the equivalent of letting mercenaries loose on campus. We were also worried that innocent students could be caught up in the crossfire, as the police had no way of differentiating between friend and foe.

The anti-riot team arrived in dramatic fashion, sirens blaring, lights flashing. As pencil is to a student, so tear gas is to anti-riot police – standard equipment, always at hand. The stench of the disabling gas spread across the school grounds. It was hard to figure out how many anti-riot police descended on our campus. But they were effective, crushing the uprising within minutes, but as we had feared, they didn't spare innocent students.

We had not seen Rex, Danksy and the other prefects since we left the Principal's house earlier that evening. I would later learn that Danksy took refuge in the house of our Physics teacher, Mr Ollo, who also supervised the drama group.

Out of nowhere, we could hear students screaming, pleading for mercy, as an anti-riot police officer lashed out at them. They had been boxed into an area between the Principal's house and the chapel. We rushed to see, from our safe perch on the balcony of the Principal's house, who had been unfortunate enough to have been caught in the anti-riot police web. There they were, three students, all lying face-down on the grass, trying desperately to cover their heads as the officer beat them mercilessly with a stick. Rex's leg was recognisable because of his vitiligo. We called to the officer to let him go, shouting that he was a prefect. He ignored us. I am not sure a loudspeaker would have made a difference.

It did not matter that we implored the Principal to pass on the message to the officer. The officer was in his own world, probably drunk. As the helpless Principal looked on, the weight of his decision to call in the anti-riot squad was crushing. But that ship had already sailed. He could only hope that no further damage was being done elsewhere on campus.

Rex was eventually released, but only after the Principal went down to appeal to the officer personally, and after the officer had flogged him to his satisfaction. Buttocks bruised and his face swollen, he stumbled into the sanctuary of the Principal's house. He had been hiding in some bushes with Sheddo, another prefect, next to the Principal's house, but decided, in his fifteen-year old wisdom, to approach the officer and try to explain that he was a prefect. The other students were not so lucky. The police took them away and locked them up in a cell until the next morning.

In addition to Rex and Sheddo, a few more students made their way to the Principal's house to seek refuge. We spent the hours that followed recounting stories of escape, heroism, horror, and deceit. No one had a good night's rest. Some slept on chairs, others on the bare floor, hoping against all odds that mosquito bites would be kept to the bare minimum.

The next morning, from our different hideouts, we made our way back to our dormitories. An uneasy calm had descended on the campus, but all around was a trail of destruction – from broken glass to mangled aluminium plates. But school life must carry on, somehow. So, the kitchen staff were back at work, setting up for breakfast. Clusters of students gathered to exchange stories from the previous night. One of these contained a group of sixth-year students – both prefects and non-prefects. There was a sense that, regardless of who was to blame, our year group, collectively, had to take responsibility for the wanton destruction. So, the entire group went to the Principal's house to apologise. When we arrived, he was a little surprised to see us. Every student in the group prostrated flat as he watched from the balcony. He kissed his teeth and retreated into his fortress. There wasn't much more to be said or done. So, we returned to the dormitories to try to pick our lives back up.

The parent teacher association (PTA) set up a committee to investigate the riot. After interviewing some non-prefects, they called the prefects in.

'Which of you is Samba?' one of them asked as we entered. Samba identified himself.

'We hear you're the prefect who goes around causing trouble'.

Samba, as usual, had been unfairly maligned by the witnesses who had given evidence to the committee. We spent the next thirty minutes explaining how we had tried to return order to the school. When they had heard enough, the Chairman addressed us.

'We were only pulling your legs. We know this school was upside down before your crop of prefects came in. It was an embarrassment to watch how young boys acted like animals around the dining hall. And all that stealing and ignoring school rules. So, we appreciate what you've done. But I want to check something with you. Are you all wearing underwear?'

This took everybody aback. Underwear?

'Sorry, sir. You mean are we wearing pants?'

'Yes, pants, underwear. Your Principal probably assumed that your suspended classmate was wearing one when he told the guard to take off his clothes. I don't think he knew the boy wasn't wearing any'.

Underwear or no underwear, the Chairman's comments didn't make us think differently of the Principal's actions. As I reflected on that disastrous night, I knew we had opened Pandora's box. Our swansong was to be this riot. All the progress made to restore order to student life had been undone, I thought. Our year group and the ensuing riot would always be linked, mentioned in the same breath, even if no one remembered what it was that triggered the event. And we could forget any valedictory or send-off events. No one in their right mind would spend a kobo on a group of students who were the root of so much destruction to school property.

The school later levied every student to raise funds for the repair bill. Apart from Oyinbo the albino, it was difficult to definitively prove who else participated in the riot. Instead, the school relied on circumstantial evidence or past behaviours, which was unfair to some students, in order to draw up a list. These students were suspended indefinitely, 'deboarded' in official language, and were permitted to return to the school grounds only to sit their exams. Also, their levy was at least double that of other students.

A sense of normalcy eventually returned to campus. During our final month on campus, several of us – boys and girls – worked together to put on a music concert that we hoped would help with the healing process. Although the concert was a success, from the perspective of the prefects, trust had been shattered. We were keen to hand over the reins to the next set, finish our exams, and say goodbye. It was a humbling experience, tumbling from the highs of just a few months prior. Our one consolation was that months of running the school properly had indoctrinated a culture of orderliness in the minds of many students on campus. The riot did not change that, even after we said our goodbyes and the SAJOMACO chapter of our lives closed. And if that was the only positive we could take away from this roller coaster experience, it was enough. We could hold our heads up high and say we did the best we could, given the circumstances, when we were called upon to serve.

Official 1996 prefects photo (Danksy and Rex missing)

Top row L-R: Seun Daramola, Yinka Orimogunje, Ibukun Adebayo (Bykes), Seyi Babawale, Tolu Onipede, Kunle Abu, Victor Lawani, Femi Adeodu, Sunkanmi Ojetayo (Jetta) and me.

Bottom row L-R: Ola Abitogun, Busayo Adeniyi (Samba), Abiodun Adanikin (Danksy), Akintade Adebori, Niyi Olorunyomi (Niyeh) and Kunle Borishade (Rex).

Epilogue

On February 28, 1991, all that mattered to me was the thought that life offered so much adventure as I started secondary school at SAJOMACO.

June 1996, when I was due to graduate, seemed back then to lie an eternity away; it was hard to contemplate ever getting there. As much as SAJOMACO promised to fill my life with fun, the spark faded and rot soon set in. A yearning for freedom would grip me for the next five years.

While I waited and persevered, there were new things to discover, cultures and norms I could not have imagined existed. Exploring life at SAJOMACO opened my eyes to the world out *there*, a world beyond that of a buttered – that is, sheltered – OAU boy. This was a world that felt unfair at times, where strange rules of respect amongst eleven- to sixteen-year-olds reigned supreme. Challenging those rules brought painful consequences. Looking back, I realised that this student culture and SAJOMACO showed me that our teachers had lives of their own, and balancing that life with their paid work was an internal conflict, one which they consistently wrestled with. They were flawed, just like we were, and being an adult didn't guarantee they couldn't be meaner than my worst nightmare at times.

SAJOMACO tested my survival skills. On campus, food was food, however disgusting the preparation process or the final product. Those nutrients just had to get inside my body. The humble pie had to be eaten. Eventually, I got used to it. Turning up one's nose, or doing *shakara* as Nigerians say, was for home, not for campus. Those survival skills also honed one's ability to look after one's belonging – to not be an ignoramus, or *suegbe*. But whether I ate, drank, and slept or not, survival beyond SAJOMACO was the greater goal. And in those days, academic performance was the best route to achieving it. Notwithstanding, Nigeria had a way of reminding one that nothing was guaranteed. Had I remained in Nigeria after leaving SAJOMACO, I probably would have been denied entry into OAU because my university entrance exam results were seized. The same fate met a few other friends from OAU. Our crime was that we had performed well – too well in fact – in one of the most difficult exams for students in Nigeria.

Over time, the longing for freedom from this prison-like SAJOMACO faded, to be replaced by the excitement of moving up the food chain as seniority beckoned. The school handed territory to a few of us – the prefects. It felt like our own mini country. Even though we have bittersweet memories, our experience gives one hope that a group of like-minded individuals might one day arrive on the national scene and make their mark, choosing to serve rather than be served, putting citizens first.

During my time at university, I established an awards scheme for the best fifth-year SAJOMACO student, the idea being that other students would see and interact with the recipients during their final year on campus. After three years of running the scheme, I shut it down because I didn't receive any feedback from the school authorities, once they received the funds. I could not confirm whether the school ran the scheme as intended or even gave the award money to the students.

A few years later, however, a student at OAU tracked down my dad at his office. Benny introduced himself and revealed that he had indeed received one of the awards and was now studying Medicine there. So, despite the lack of information from the school, the scheme had apparently run, even if the details were sketchy. That was encouraging. Benny would go on to achieve excellent results. Sadly, he, too, joined the brain drain that is Nigeria's greatest export, heading to the United Kingdom after securing a well-paid job as a doctor.

SAJOMACO scarred some people for life. As a classmate told me later, 'hurt people end up hurting other people'. The riot was only a window into that, and the ramifications have continued till this very day for our year group. After the funeral of SAJOMACO's first Principal in late 2020 – the man who had given the *cantab* order in my first year at the dining hall, a few alumni commented that my year group was notably underrepresented at the event.

Some illusions grew after SAJOMACO; others were shattered. People change. Difficult, probably misunderstood, students became respectable adults; some Pharisee equivalent proved to be non-immune to moral decay after all. A few students have died – sometimes tragically, some allegedly through suicide. Many are married, some to SAJOMACO classmates, despite not having shown any interest in each other during their time on campus. Some have separated from their spouses, and others are divorced. Some were cheated on; others barren. Some well-to-do students currently live in penury, whilst some students from poorer backgrounds are now affluent enough to employ their seniors, many times over.

Given the opportunity, would I change aspects of my SAJOMACO experience? Maybe. It is tempting, I admit.

But then without this adventure – the survival of which continues to pay dividends to this very day – I risk diluting the richness, the messiness, the colourful past that framed my identity.

Acknowledgements

They say it takes a village to raise a child. That is how I feel at the end of this project. Without these 'villagers', it would have been impossible to cross the finish line. I am forever indebted to:

My wife, Tosin, for her unrelenting support throughout the entire process, and our children, Tadelicious, Simstar and Kolestik, for tolerating me while this work consumed my life

My parents, for taking a risk by sending me (and my brothers) to SAJOMACO, and for editing and fact-checking my manuscript

Jide Olanrewaju, Paul Adams, Rele Adesina, Bodunrin Sasore, Abimbola Alaba and Ioana Danaila for the precious hours they gave up to support this endeavour

My very own special task force - Lola Smith, David Smith, Victoria Omopariola, Ebun Edwin, Joseph Lasore - who sacrificed countless hours editing, debating, correcting and grilling me, doubling as a survey group and more, to bring the best out of this project

Marie Asaolu, Yemi Asaolu, Tega Sofoluke, Michael Sofoluke, Franchesca Gerald, Berna Holmes, Andrew Holmes and ADot the Comedian for being 'yes people' to my multimedia requests

Fina Asaolu, Wole Asaolu, Atinuke Williams, Femi Omopari-ola, Solomon Edwin, Jumoke Okeowo, Nicole Kanu, JR Kanu, Tosin Taiwo, Nneoma Ikema-Williams, Mitch Ikema-Williams and Mummy Omolara Lasore for their invaluable feedback and moral support

Dan Lees, Tharshish Johnson and Emmanuel Olaleye for being a sounding board and making themselves available when I needed a different perspective

SAJOMACO colleagues who helped with factual accuracy and many of my requests - Ibukun Adebayo, Tayo Okunade, Femi Adeodu, Osagie Agboh, Tope Fayose, Tope Dahunsi, Biodun Adanikin, Kazeem Ojomo, Kunle Borishade, Sunkanmi Oje-tayo, Ola Abitogun, Tunde Omoloja, Busayo Adeniyi, Seyi Babawale, Niyi Olorunyomi and Seun Daramola. Special thanks to Tomisin Giwa for going above and beyond the call of duty

Jada Badu-Animboah, Derrick Amoako, Henrietta Fosu-Mensah, Mope Oyetunji and Lolade Sasore for dragging their personal network into this project

Jola Ayeye, Barbara Ezeife, Violet Phiri, Tosin Ajayi, Tayo Lanlehin, Dolu Lanlehin, Teni Olatunde, Tomi Oloko, Yomi Oloko, Tolu Akinyosoye, Chidiogo Nwosu, Kingston Nwosu, Temi Okeowo, Gbolade Okeowo, Yinka Osaji, Leke Olabiran,

Tayo Fadipe, Chinwe Egwim, Rolake Akinkugbe-Filani, Bim Oyetade, Abi Oyetade, Miracle Ewim, Bukky Shobowale, Deji Shobowale, Anu Adasolum, Ire Aderinokun, Oris Aigbokhaevbolo, Kristin Wilson, IB Adedugbe, Lola Dansu, Bunmi Alli, Sade Akhanoba, Busola Oladimeji, Chiamaka Sowemimo, Eneh Jones, Funto Amire, Nnenna Onuba, Ugo Arinzeh, Ijeoma Agboti-Obatoyinbo for responding to my many requests at various points on this journey

Rafael Andres for capturing the essence of the odyssey with the cover design

Adriano Bezerra for bringing the SAJOMACO map to life

Siobhan Gallagher, my copyeditor, for upgrading my manuscript, and Gregory Kronsten, for proofreading and more

And finally, Reedsy and Canva, for empowering me throughout this journey.

Praise for Surviving SAJOMACO

This is a book which I wish I had read before moving to Nigeria. The author's account of life in a boarding school there gives a rare insight into Nigeria's way of life. It describes the power of people in authority and the lack of respect they command, as the pupils adhere rigidly to the rules yet strive to subvert them. The hardship and insecurity Nigerians suffered in the 1990s as the military regime clung to power was widely documented. There are few accounts of the effects on an academic community during this turbulent time. The fate of the school is a microcosm of the simultaneous decline of Nigeria's professional classes, leading to a brain drain to the developed world that has included the author.

Paul Adams, Former Financial Times Nigeria Correspondent

A genuine, scrupulously honest insight into day-to-day life in a Nigerian boarding school during a tumultuous period for the country. Bunmi manages to capture, in exquisite detail, the sometimes shocking, and occasionally unbelievable, reality many of us endured. A brave and necessary book.

'Jide Olanrewaju, Vice Chairman, Royal African Society; Writer & Producer of Naij, A History of Nigeria

In order to chart a course forward to a desired location from an undesirable one, it is useful to know where we are presently and, better still, have some clarity about how we got there. Nations are born of and built by people. Bunmi's book gives very important insights into the psyche of Nigeria's young middle class and how this psyche was constructed. The book helps to explain how we got here and should help us to figure out how to leave. If this nation is to come into its own, leave we must!

Rele Adesina, Former Commissioner for Budget and Planning, Ogun State, Nigeria; granddaughter of Aya Mase

Surviving SAJOMACO isn't a book; it's a necessary journey, enjoyably retracing the identity of a generation. Bunmi Asaolu's fountain pen dips deep into the rich ink of nostalgia. An adult bedtime story that will leave you dreaming far away from 2021. This grown man's memory is authentically through a child's eyes. If you are Nigerian, it is a must-read for reconnection; if you are not Nigerian, a must-read for context. Funny, I didn't realise Asaolu and I went to the same boarding school. Apparently we all did; it's called SAJOMACO.

Bodunrin Sasore, Award Winning Filmmaker

A beautifully written memoir that gives the reader a glimpse into the weight and the limits of education and culture. However tough his experience might have been, Asaolu's writing remains nonjudgmental without lacking distance. The account he gives is much more factual than critical so as to present SAJOMACO as a place that builds character as much as a high academic level, and therefore creates the space for debate.

Ioana Danaila, The African Book Review

Surviving SAJOMACO is testament of harsh realities, and Bunmi Asaolu's incredible command of the past dumps his readers into the emotions evoked by a vivid retelling of events. In a well nuanced use of language, Bunmi explores the tragicomedies of boarding school life in Nigeria with spirited grace. He knits several strands of narrative—education, politics and culture— together with the intricacy of finely woven tapestry. This work is a victory of memory and Bunmi exposes the larger truth of Nigeria and charts its incongruous growth as a nation through an account of the highs and lows of a schoolboy's life. This is an honest but often alarming exposition into solidarity and brotherhood, into culture, faith and the use and abuse of power. This is an important and necessary book, and a thoroughly engrossing read.

Abimbola Alaba, Author of The Revolution Generation

About the Author

Bunmi Asaolu was born in Ile-Ife, Nigeria in 1980 but joined the brain drain out of Nigeria in 1996 with his family. After completing his Chemical Engineering degree at Imperial College London, the allure of the City of London was stronger than working at a chemical plant. So, he wrote investment research on European technology companies for a few years at the now infamous Lehman Brothers until its collapse in 2008. Post-Lehman, he pivoted to advising investment managers in Europe, South Africa and the United States on Nigeria. He has a life outside banking though. He sings and plays the keyboard for his church band and, with his wife, Tosin, helps reduce the global divorce case count by counselling young married couples. In his spare time, he forcefully schools their three children in mathematics.

@thebunmiasaolu (Instagram, LinkedIn, Twitter, YouTube)
www.bunmiasaolu.com

Printed in Great Britain
by Amazon